LEAD WITH
VALUE

Lead With Value

A Blueprint for Leading with Purpose and Impact

Bruce Cardenas

Published by Game Changer Publishing

Cover Design: Skylar Ringenbach

Disclaimer: This book is a work of narrative nonfiction. Names, identifying characteristics, and details have been changed to protect privacy. Any resemblance to actual persons is coincidental.

Paperback ISBN: 979-8-90158-405-7

Hardcover ISBN: 979-8-90158-060-8

Digital ISBN: 979-8-90158-061-5

www.GameChangerPublishing.com

To my parents, Jon and Mary Cardenas, for their unwavering love and life's teachings that helped pave the way and forge the path for me to become the man I am today.

TESTIMONIALS

I had the pleasure of having Bruce as a guest speaker at our Secret Knock private event in San Diego. What a pleasure getting to know him and hearing his story as a servant, leader, and next-level brand builder. Bruce's approach of bringing value to others with no expectation in return is a very unique trait rarely found in people. Respect and admiration for what he has accomplished in building billion-dollar brands.

Greg Reid
Author, *Think and Grow Rich:*
Stickability, The Power of Perseverance

Bruce's relationship expertise fundamentally changed how I view connection and inspired Rule No. 2 of The Few: "To get, give." He created the roadmap for building authentic relationships with no expectations. If you want to scale your brand or maximize your impact, listen to Bruce.

Joey Bowen
Founder of Few Will Hunt

I've known Bruce for over 15 years. He has helped me immensely to build and scale two very successful companies. Bruce has trained himself to always be on the lookout for marketing opportunities that other people don't see. Perhaps his strongest asset is that he inspires others to do this in a way that's not only authentic but also keeps the best interests of the people he engages with at the forefront.

Ron Penna
Founder of Quest Nutrition and
Legendary Foods, entrepreneur

Over the years, I've watched Bruce build brands, share knowledge, and forge relationships like no one I have ever seen before. His passion for bringing value to other people comes through with every engagement you will witness.

Jay Cutler
Four-time Mr. Olympia
champion, entrepreneur

You won't find another person as genuine or as willing to help, support, and mentor you through his lifetime of experiences as Bruce Cardenas. A true example of what being a servant leader is all about. Warren Buffett once said, "It takes twenty years to build a relationship and five minutes to ruin it." Bruce is one of those rare individuals whose reputation precedes him. Every single person who knows Bruce will tell you about his incredible work ethic. Servant, heart, and kindness towards others.

Bedros Keuilian
Author, coach, business
owner, and entrepreneur

From the moment I met Bruce, I knew he was someone special. He carries a true servant's heart—always showing up with love, inspiration, and unwavering support. He doesn't just talk about leadership; he embodies it. I invited him to be a part of my annual events because of who he is at his core: full of integrity, generosity, and compassion. The ripple effect of his kindness and presence is felt by everyone fortunate enough to cross his path. His life is proof that when you lead with value, you create impact that stretches far beyond what you can see.

Amberly Lago
USA Today bestselling author, TEDx
speaker, podcast host, and coach

Bruce Cardenas is truly a diamond in the rough. What sets Bruce apart is his ability to give freely of his wisdom and knowledge, always helping others conquer whatever they set their minds to. He is a master communicator, a leader who knows how to take companies from the ground floor and build them into multimillion-dollar industries. Beyond the accolades, Bruce is one of the most humble, easygoing badasses I've ever met. He's been there for me in times of need, no matter how busy his schedule is. We need more people like Bruce Cardenas in this world.

Ray Cash Care
Former Navy SEAL, Peak Performance
Coach, Great American

I've known Bruce since the 1990s, and he is a paradox in the best sense: a highly skilled special operator and the kind of gentleman you want to hang out with. What makes his story compelling is how uniquely qualified he is to handle the toughest situations while carrying himself with grace and humanity. He's also the friend you call when you just need someone to listen—he hears you fully, without judgment. Over the years, he's become more than a friend—he's a mentor. Extremely talented with a steady presence, I find myself striving to be more like him.

Charlie Horky
Founder of CLS Worldwide
Transportation, entrepreneur

What hit me about Bruce's message is how simple, but powerful, it is: Lead with value and give with generosity, every single day. That's not just business talk; that's survival and legacy. His way of building relationship capital is real, and it's a skill anybody can use to turn their life around, whether you're chasing a championship, building a business, or rebuilding after going down the wrong path. In my journey from a drug kingpin to a man who now moves with purpose, I see Bruce as a living example of what happens when you lead with intention and authenticity.

Owen Hanson
Cocaine Quarterback (documentary), entrepreneur,
founder of California Ice Protein

Bruce's approach to leading with value is so unique, yet such a simple thing we can all do better: to give with generosity and do it daily. This one thing is how he's been a master of relationship capital, a skill that everyone needs to enroll others into their dreams and goals. In my book *Unicorn Team* (Penguin, 2025), I profile Bruce's story because it's a real example of how to share your authenticity with people you want to do life and business with, just by being someone who leads with intention.

Jen Kem
CEO of Master Brand, Inc.

READ THIS FIRST

Just to say thanks for buying and reading my book,
I would like to connect!
Scan the QR Code Here:

LEAD WITH VALUE

A BLUEPRINT
FOR LEADING WITH
PURPOSE AND IMPACT

BRUCE CARDENAS

FOREWORD

There are some people you meet in life who are more than acquaintances, more than even friends—they become examples. They remind you that resilience and vision are not just words, but ways of living. My friend Bruce Cardenas is one of those people.

From the first time I met Bruce, I knew he was the real deal. No pretense, no drama, no performance—just a man deeply grounded in his purpose and ignited by passion. I often say to others, "Don't be a discount version of yourself," and Bruce embodies that fully. He shows up as his authentic self.

Before Bruce was in the boardrooms and building brands, he was a Marine. Then an LAPD officer. And those who've walked through those callings know that they're not just jobs. They're missions. They demand grit, discipline, and a level of selflessness that few choose. That foundation shaped the way Bruce moves through every chapter of his life: with a courage that is steady, and with a servant heart that is open.

When Bruce stepped into the world of business, he didn't come with all the connections or a polished résumé. But what he did come with was vision, perseverance, and an unstoppable commitment to people. At Quest Nutrition and later through Legendary Foods, Bruce didn't just build companies. He built bridges. He created cultures. He led with value, not just with words, but with action.

You've heard me say before, "A comeback isn't a go back," and Bruce's story proves that truth. He never tried to return to what was; he created what could be. Each season of his life has been about moving forward—Marine to officer, officer to entrepreneur, entrepreneur to mentor. His comeback was always about becoming his utmost self, not getting stuck in an almost life.

And here's what I love most: Bruce leads with desire, but he always backs it up with discipline. I teach that when you have desire, you must have discipline to get to your destination. Bruce has lived that out in front of us all. His consistency is what has turned his dreams into a reality and his influence into impact.

Lead With Value is not just a blueprint for leadership. It's a reflection of Bruce himself—a life lived with courage, integrity, and compassion. As you turn these pages, you'll find practical wisdom. You'll find strategy. But more than that, you'll find heart.

Bruce is proof that leadership is not about a title or position. It's about how you make people feel, how you lift them, how you stand for them. It's about impact that lasts beyond the room you're in.

So lean in. Take notes. But more importantly, take it to heart. Because this isn't just Bruce's story. It's an invitation for your own. To live fully. To lead with value. To never settle for being a discount version of yourself, but to rise into the fullness of who you were created to be.

Tim Storey
Coach, speaker, and author of *The Miracle Mentality*

CONTENTS

HONOR

COURAGE

COMMITMENT

INTRODUCTION

When I was in the third grade, I suffered a tragic accident. My classmate and I were on the school bus heading home, and the driver let us off at the wrong stop. When we realized it, we ran to catch up with the bus at the next stop, but we missed it. My friend and I then had to cross a four-lane intersection by ourselves. The crossing guard gave us the okay to cross, and we sprinted off. We made it across three lanes when, halfway through the fourth, we were struck by a taxi. There were no cell phones at the time, but someone managed to call an ambulance, and we were rushed to the emergency room.

That was a really scary experience. I was in a lot of pain, but I also remember feeling embarrassed that they were cutting my clothes off to take a look at the damage. My leg was broken in four places, and my kidneys were severely injured. I was in a cast from my toes to my hip. Tragically, my classmate died in that accident. I was thankful to be alive. Due to my injuries, I was limited in the things I was capable of doing on my own. I was in a full leg cast and on crutches for the rest of the year. I missed a lot of school. Eventually, my parents and teachers decided to make the difficult decision to hold me back a year, and I repeated third grade.

The accident set in motion a domino effect. It was a really difficult thing to go through at such a young age. I struggled in my classes; my grades were pretty much straight D's and F's from then on out. Technically, my confidence should have plummeted. Getting handed back failed tests, quizzes, and homework every week for years was basically like receiving rejection after rejection, or like that word we all hate so much, "No" after "No." As it turns out, the more you're told "No," the less you fear it. It was as if I had suffered so many failures that I had quite literally become immune to them. Grades were just grades, and somewhere deep down, I knew that I was smart, regardless of the letters on my papers. In many ways, that accident shaped the person I became for the better.

I think a parent's typical response to their kid bringing home failed test after failed test would involve a ton of scolding, punishment, and shaming their kid for their lack of effort. But this wasn't your typical situation, and my dad wasn't your typical dad. My failed tests never meant that I had failed as a person, and my father never let my grades define my potential. Even though I was a terrible student, he was my biggest cheerleader. No matter what grades I brought home, he'd look at me with the same pride because he never stopped believing in me. He would remind me of my special personality, my smile, and my unique laugh, which made other people laugh.

I would be remiss if I didn't mention my mother. She, unfortunately, was an alcoholic early on in my life. I often saw my mom fast asleep on the couch with a glass in her hand and two empty wine bottles on the table. When we came home from school and Dad from work, she always made dinner so that we could eat together. But at night, once we were asleep, she had no more fight left in her, and she gave in to her addiction.

My siblings and I were too young to truly grasp the reality of our situation, so it fell to my father to carry it alone. He never failed to provide the essentials for us, and we always had a roof over our heads, food on the table, and a bed to sleep in. He stood up to the challenge that almost broke our family apart—and did so with a smile—so his kids would never have to know what their parents were going through.

The terrifying thing about addictions is how difficult they can be to get yourself out of, as they can be hidden in plain sight. My mother must have had someone watching over her because thankfully—some way, somehow—she made her way to recovery and AA meetings. After my mother was officially sober and fully recovered, she landed a job with my school board. She remains sober to this day. This change turned her entire life around and saved her marriage, her family, and possibly even her life. I couldn't be prouder of her. Although it was her personal challenge, it affected us all. I witnessed how deeply it affected her and vowed never to drink in my life.

I can attribute the early lessons I learned from my father, who was an important influence in my life, to my becoming the successful businessperson I am today. He was a workaholic, which some today might refer to as an entrepreneur. He started his own electrical contracting business. He took it upon himself to teach me what I like to call "perishable life skills." Perishable skills are skills that can be lost if not practiced, such as building fires, which I learned as a Boy Scout. The perishable life skills my dad taught me focused on responsibility as I grew up. Living on the East Coast, we experienced all four seasons, and my dad helped us look at each as a business opportunity.

In the spring, we mowed our neighbors' lawns. For years, my younger brother, Brian, and I, along with a couple of friends, would go door-to-door to see what our neighbors needed help with. In the summer, we washed cars and cleaned windows. In the fall, we raked leaves, and in the winter, when it was freezing cold and nobody wanted to leave their houses, we shoveled snow from driveways and walkways, and we chopped wood for fireplaces. This didn't make us teenage billionaires by any means. But with five kids in our group, the cash started adding up. I guess we were doing side hustles long before side hustles became a trend or even a commonly known term.

There was only one rule that my father made us stick to: we didn't charge our elderly neighbors. One of those neighbors was a nice lady named Mrs. Hoffman. We would shovel her snow, rake her leaves, and even cut her grass occasionally. She never once paid us, but she always baked us delicious treats to enjoy after our hard work. Many of our elderly neighbors "paid" us this way.

When I was a kid, I'm sure I would've appreciated the extra five bucks, but looking back now, I appreciate the lesson even more. They were physically unable to do the tasks we were offering, and we were more than capable of lending a helping hand. My father taught me so much about hard work, respecting others, and giving back.

Fast forward to when I was nineteen years old, and we were getting ready to sit down to family dinner when there was a knock on the door. It was Mrs. Hoffman's son, who was probably 40 years old at the time. We didn't really know him well, but he told us that his mother had passed away the month prior. We had seen the obituary in our hometown newspaper. He handed my brother and me each an envelope.

He went on to say that his mother was always grateful for what we did for her and that she had been on a very fixed pension and didn't have a lot of money. As her health was declining, she asked her son to give us these envelopes and thanked us for the years of taking care of her without being compensated with money. In each envelope was $500 in cash and a little card with the Lord's Prayer. After he left, my father smiled at us and said, "Now you understand."

When I was a child, I didn't realize the value of seeing my parents' actions and choices—of watching my mother recover from alcoholism and watching my father be a strong leader in business. They showed me the importance of taking care of yourself and looking out for others. I have carried those lessons far in my life. Throughout my career and entrepreneurial endeavors, I have always remembered the value of investing in the people I hire and treating them with respect. I have always remembered the value in showing up for myself and others, even when it's difficult. These are some of the most underrated building blocks on your way to success.

I grew up just a regular kid, the middle child of five, in a blue-collar town in New Jersey. Both of my parents worked my entire childhood. We weren't poor, but we weren't rich either. I struggled through school, just like a lot of kids. I became a police officer, which was a childhood dream of mine. I served in the United States Marine Corps, I launched my own bodyguard business, and I played a critical role in the growth of Quest Nutrition. While I've been very successful and benefited financially from all the hard work, it hasn't been easy. I went through a divorce. I suffered financial hardships when I first started my bodyguard business. I worked long, hard hours—for free at the beginning—to carve out my place at Quest Nutrition.

I did all of this because I wanted to. I was motivated to live a life that is meaningful to me. I think a lot of people are looking for ways to become a better person in both their personal and professional lives. Maybe you're an entrepreneur, a business owner, or a CEO. Maybe you're not sure what you want to do with your life. Maybe you're considering starting a business or even a side hustle. If you have a dream that you want to achieve, you're in the right place.

In this book, I share my failures and my successes, and how I learned to succeed and be confident despite my poor showing in school. I share tips and advice on growing your business while keeping your purpose at the forefront of everything you do. I teach you how to foster a positive work culture and build meaningful relationships with employees, coworkers, customers, and buyers. I help you not only avoid the landmines that I encountered but also understand the most important building blocks to a successful business. I've learned a lot of lessons in my life, both from setbacks and successes. I want to share these lessons with you.

My goal in writing this book is to give you some tools to become a better person and, in turn, a better leader—whether a manager, a business owner, an employee, or a CEO. I hope you find inspiration and actionable takeaways that motivate you to go after your dreams.

A NOTE ABOUT QUEST NUTRITION

Several famous authors and poets have said, "If you're going to write your story, make sure you're holding the pen." I am holding the pen to share my personal memories with Quest Nutrition—an experience that I talk about in this book.

Many people have written their own versions of the events that took place at Quest Nutrition. There have been individuals claiming to be part of Quest Nutrition whom I have never heard of or met and who, to the best of my knowledge, were never involved with the company. I've also heard people speak publicly about accomplishments they achieved "on their own," taking full credit for something they could not have achieved without the founding members' involvement.

I would like to share the most accurate facts from the beginning, including the story behind Quest Nutrition. The following information is verified by Quest Nutrition founders Ron Penna and Mike Osborn, Shannan Penna, who developed the original recipes in her kitchen, and Quest Nutrition partner, Michael Veni.

In 2008, Shannan Penna—whose Instagram handle is @questcreator—began making protein bars in her kitchen to share with her girlfriends and clients, the latter of whom she coached and trained in her fitness boot camps. Her husband, Ron, owned a successful security software company with his business partner, Mike Osborn. Ron and Mike Osborn have been entrepreneurs since their college days, having attempted to launch some twenty-odd businesses—most of which were unsuccessful—over the years.

Ron happened to be looking for a side hustle. He was in talks with a well-known bodybuilder in Los Angeles about starting a supplement company together. At the same time, he saw something in Shannan's protein bars and brought them to work to share with his employees. Everyone really enjoyed them and started regularly asking for more.

That's when he had a lightbulb moment, realizing that his next business opportunity was actually much closer to home. He pitched his idea to his closest associates—Mike Osborn, Michael Veni, and Tom Bilyeu—about starting a protein bar company. At first, the idea didn't go over well with everyone. Ron's associates reminded him that they were in the tech space, not the nutrition space.

Fortunately, Ron did not give up that easily. He enlisted the help of Michael Veni, who worked behind the scenes to build a website and hire food scientists who tweaked Shannan's recipes to create test samples that would ensure a stable shelf life. They shared these samples with family and friends, and the interest grew from there.

They went back to Mike Osborn and the others with more data and positive feedback from those who had tried the new bar samples. This time around, they convinced them to join the endeavor. I do want to add the caveat that Ron and Mike Osborn financially funded Quest Nutrition—no one else. In its fifth year, an outside equity firm invested in the company and then helped sell Quest Nutrition to Simply Good Foods, a publicly traded company, in 2019.

Shannan continued testing new recipes at home in her kitchen. She was responsible for the first fourteen flavors launched at Quest Nutrition. Ron, Mike Osborn, Michael Veni, and Tom Bilyeu would take the recipes and, with the help of a few seasoned food scientists and some encouraging ingredient suppliers, scale them for commercial production. They transitioned to making the bars in a kitchen commissary on evenings and weekends, while still working their tech jobs during the day.

The business was officially launched in 2010 under the name Quest Protein Bar. They changed the name to Quest Nutrition shortly after launching. Over time, many people came and went through the doors of Quest Nutrition, with some executives and partners departing (a nice way of saying some people got fired) before the eventual sale of the company.

At the time of sale, Ron and Mike Osborn were the only two founders still at the company. A small group of us was also fortunate enough to be part of the equity pool and benefit from a $1 billion cash sale. Yeah! A privately owned startup company valued at $1 billion or more is known as a "unicorn" in business. Quest Nutrition was the first of its kind in the "better for you" nutrition space.

One year before the sale of Quest Nutrition, Ron approached the investment firm and the board of directors to get their permission to develop a new side business. He started this side hustle in 2015 with Michael Veni, and it was a company called Legendary Foods. In the beginning, they focused primarily on seasoned nuts and uniquely flavored nut butters to avoid any conflict with Quest Nutrition while still being able to exist in the low-carb nutrition space. Over the next few years, Ron and Michael Veni worked tirelessly to formulate products and build a team to get Legendary Foods off the ground. I joined them at the start to help build the team at Legendary Foods while I was still transitioning out of working at Quest Nutrition. The early days of Legendary Foods were much like those of Quest Nutrition. When I first started with the team, we were working in a kitchen commissary in Pasadena. Legendary Foods has now expanded, commercially scaling a variety of snacks that are high in protein and low in carbs and sugar.

And that's the high-level story of Quest Nutrition. I talk quite a bit about my journey there throughout this book, and I wanted to start with this note on how the company came to be, how it was sold, and how Ron and Michael Veni transitioned to leading Legendary Foods with a new and revolutionary approach to snacks.

CHAPTER 1
ANCHORING YOURSELF IN PURPOSE

Growing up, I had a dream: to become a police officer. It's common for boys to have the idea that they are going to be a police officer, a fireman, an astronaut, or a scientist. Those are all boyhood fantasies.

I had multiple people I looked up to and admired who were in the police force. One was my uncle, who was a decorated police veteran in Philadelphia and died in the line of duty. My neighbor was a colonel with the New Jersey State Police. My older sister dated a police officer and ultimately married him. I saw the sense of fulfillment they felt in giving back to the community through their careers as police officers. They were incredible mentors.

When I was in high school, the local police department knew me. They were a five-person department, and it was a very small town. Everybody knew everybody. They knew my older brother because he was always getting in trouble with the police. He hung out on "the other side of town" and regularly got arrested for minor things, like drugs and trespassing. They knew me as the athletic younger brother. In high school, they would let me do ride-alongs, and that was when I knew that becoming a police officer was what I wanted to do with my life. They even issued me a uniform that I wore while patrolling with them.

I had this dream, this vision, but I didn't have a clear path to get there. I was a 'C' and 'D' student at best; I didn't really care much about applying myself. A week before graduating high school, I got my grades and learned that I had failed one of my classes. At the time, my mom served on the school board's transportation committee, and she came home that day pretty upset. She was never stern like this, and I remember the conversation very clearly. She made sure I was listening before she started talking. She told me, "Bruce, I got a call from your principal today. Did you know that you failed your final exam in Mr. Hoist's class? You're short of the credits you need to graduate. You can't walk with your friends next week at graduation."

At the time, I didn't really understand the impact of failing a class and not being able to graduate. I nearly dismissed it until my mom said, "Bruce, you need to understand something. You have this dream of being a police officer, right? That won't happen if you don't have a high school diploma. No matter how much you want it or how hard you work for it, they legally can not hire you without it. A high school diploma is the basis for anything you want to do, Bruce. And you're going to have to go to summer school."

I resisted at first. I told her I'd go out and find work, that I could figure it out and become a cop one day. She said, "No, seriously, you will not become a police officer without a high school degree. And I'm adamant; you must go to summer school."

She never talked to me like that. I let it sink in, and I was devastated. One of my biggest aspirations and lifelong dreams since I was a little boy was at stake. The road to becoming a police officer looked unreachable for me. Not to mention it was embarrassing that I couldn't walk at graduation. My girlfriend was the star of the high school basketball team, and she had passed all her classes with honors —and here I was, not even able to graduate.

The denial faded and quickly turned into motivation. I attended summer school and earned my diploma. My dream wasn't at risk anymore. But, for the next year or so, I floundered around town, holding miscellaneous jobs, not really sure what I was going to do. The police were still letting me do ride-alongs with them. The police chief of a neighboring town asked me if I'd like to start working for him on Saturdays and Sundays. He had his own side hustle business as a farrier, shoeing horses at the local ranches. The chief needed extra help on busy days, and I jumped at the chance to make extra money. Once I got to know the chief on a more personal level, I finally mustered up enough courage to approach him with a question.

I went to him one day and said, "Chief, I really want to join the High Bridge Police Department—or any police department, really. It's my goal. I've been out of school for almost two years. I'm ready. What do I need to do to accomplish it?"

I had no idea what it meant to be a police officer. I knew I enjoyed the ride-alongs and that people I looked up to, like my uncle, were fulfilled by their work. The chief gave it to me straight in his own kind words and said, "Bruce, you're young, you're dumb, and you're imma-ture. I know you barely squeaked out of high school. But if you go into the Marine Corps, as I did when I was a young man, I'll hire you the day you get out." I don't remember if he actually called me dumb, but that was my takeaway from the conversation. I still had a lot to learn before becoming a police officer.

I processed that and said, "Okay, great, thank you very much." I left that conversation feeling insecure and in fear of the unknown because all I knew was High Bridge, New Jersey. I was confused why he wanted me to leave the only place I knew, only to return one day. I couldn't get my head around that. I was so comfortable in High Bridge. A few weeks turned into a few months, and I still found myself stuck in my same old routine, working a day job and doing ride-alongs. I started getting embarrassed whenever I saw the chief. He never brought it up again, but the opportunity was still on the table; I just hadn't acted on it.

One Sunday, I woke up in a panic, feeling like my window to become a police officer was getting smaller and smaller by the day. I heard the church bells ringing down the street. The house I grew up in was a block away from the Catholic church where we attended mass and Sunday School and where I had my First Communion. At the end of that Sunday's service, I hung back to talk to the priest. He was saying goodbye to everyone as they left. He paused when he got to me and said, "Bruce, to what do I owe the pleasure? I've never seen you or your brother stick around."

We went outside to sit on a bench, and I began to explain. "Well, not too long ago, I received an opportunity from the chief. He told me he will hire me one day if I go into the Marine Corps first. But I really don't know what to do. I'm quite comfortable in High Bridge, but I also feel like I'm falling into this hole that I'll never be able to get out of."

The priest chuckled and nodded. He paused for a second and said, "I'll be right back." When he came back outside again, he was holding a wooden box that looked like something you'd keep souvenirs in. With the box placed on his lap, he said to me, "Bruce, the chief is right. You need to go into the Marine Corps. It'll be the best thing for you." As he was talking, he opened up the box and took out what appeared to be a medal of some kind. I couldn't tell what it was. He admitted, "I've been holding onto this for a long time," and he put it into my hand.

The priest continued, explaining that it was St. Michael's Medallion. He told me, "St. Michael is a protector of first responders and military people. You're going to join the Marine Corps, but you're not going to come back to New Jersey. You see, there's something about you. I've watched you grow up for years, Bruce. Everyone likes you. You have great energy. Naturally, everyone gravitates towards you. There's going to be a greater calling for you in life, I promise you, and the Marine Corps is the answer. Believe me, I hope you come back and visit us, but you won't be coming back to live and work because there are greater things out there for you."

We found ourselves at the Marine Corps recruitment office the next week. The recruiter who greeted us was in full uniform. I was sold the minute I walked through those doors. After we filled out hours' worth of paperwork, he asked me what I wanted to do. I said, "Well, I want to join the military because I want to come out of this ready to take my next step as a police officer." He said, "Great! The next thing you'll do is fill out a basic aptitude test." When he said "test," I immediately panicked. Mind you, I was the kid who failed third grade, was held back a year, didn't get my high school diploma with the rest of the class, and then had to go to summer school. He could tell by my face that I was nervous. He reassured me, "It's not a big deal at all. It's just some multiple-choice questions. Everybody passes it."

When I finished the test and handed it back to him, he looked at it, then at the answer sheet, and then at my test again. I could see the numbers, and I could tell the answers weren't lining up. Plus, I could see it in his face that it was not good. To be honest, half of my answers were just guesses. "So, what did you want to do again?" he asked. My answer never changed: "I want to eventually be a police officer."

With ease, he said, "Don't worry about your test; let's get you in boot camp. We'll get you in the Marine Corps and work out what you'll do later on." He was an amazing salesman. As a matter of fact, I think he probably could have worked at QVC selling knives—he was that good. I was already sold on going to the Marine Corps. I bought into the experience, believing him wholeheartedly, and didn't worry about the test.

Next thing you know, my journey with the Marine Corps had begun. We went to Parris Island, South Carolina, for training. I had never been on an airplane in my life. Up to this point, I felt like I had been a burden on society, in a way, and now I was finally experiencing something big. Training was hard. Parris Island is best depicted by the movie *Full Metal Jacket*. That's truly the best way I could describe the experience. It was hot; there were swamps and sand fleas, and they worked us to the bone. I lost thirty pounds during boot camp. I went into the Marine Corps as a young boy and came out a grown man.

In the Marine Corps, I learned about work ethic and responsibility— from simple things like making my bed every morning to more complicated tasks like maintaining my equipment. The most important thing I learned was the Marine Corps' core values of honor, courage, and commitment. I'd never heard of the idea of core values before, and these really resonated with me. Those words became the foundation for the rest of my life. Since then, I've added my own core values: integrity, a solid moral compass, work ethic, and focus. These values have remained at the center of everything I do, both personally and professionally.

I remember when my parents came to my graduation; they hardly recognized me. I was strong and disciplined, calling everyone "sir" and "ma'am." It was the first time I truly saw pride in my parents' eyes. I'm not saying they weren't proud of me when I was a kid, but I could tell they acknowledged that this was quite an achievement for me. My dad was not very vocal; he was quiet and led by example. He didn't often say much, but that day he said, "I'm really proud of you for being able to accomplish this. There's always been something about you, Bruce. I know you're going to do great things."

My experience in the Marine Corps honestly changed my life and put me on a trajectory to where I am today. If I hadn't gone, I don't think all the things that happened in my life after that would have happened at all. I went from being that kid who was failing academically in New Jersey to being a leader at one of the largest nutrition companies in the world.

I recently attended a mastermind where I was a speaker, along with several others. One of the main speakers was a former Navy SEAL. During his presentation, he shared a very interesting statistic. He said that a high percentage of military personnel participated in wrestling, track and field, football, and swimming when they were younger.

This truly made me reflect on my childhood and my relationship with my father. Even though we were lower-middle-class, my father still got us involved in all kinds of activities, including wrestling, football, and Little League. He bought me my first gun—a 22 Mossberg bolt-action rifle—at eleven years old. I got involved in shooting in our small local NRA chapter. Those shooting skills proved priceless when I found myself on Parris Island for Marine Corps boot camp. I was one of the best shots in my unit. So many things I learned in my youth made that part of the training stress-free. Many recruits are scared to death of possibly drowning in the advanced water training in the Marine Corps. I wasn't worried one bit. I reflected on my years of swimming in Lake Solitude, jumping off the dam, and being a thrill seeker in the water. My comfort and confidence in the water meant that I had no fear of that intense training during boot camp.

My father never talked about his time in the military and the injuries he sustained in an explosion. I suspect he learned many perishable life skills he taught me as a kid while he was in the military. He was the Jocko Willink of the '70s and '80s.

My father was our Boy Scout leader, and through him, I was exposed to many opportunities that other kids didn't have. We hiked fifty miles of the Appalachian Trail every summer, starting in a different section each year so that each hike would be unique and require different skill sets. He taught us how to make our own beef jerky, purify water, and tie various knots with ropes. We also went rappelling and spelunking (cave exploring). All the kids in the neighborhood wanted to hang out at our house and do activities with my dad. He lived life to the fullest, sharing many cool experiences with me and my friends.

As an adult, I recognize the priceless lessons that he taught me. But as a teenager, I did not fully appreciate my dad. It's typical to go through three phases of life with your parents. When we're young, we idolize them. During our teen years, we tend to demonize them. And once we're adults, we finally humanize them. My dad taught me how to be an entrepreneur before I knew what the word meant. I'm grateful that my father was able to see me have some level of financial and business success. He passed away from colon cancer at the age of sixty-one.

I clearly remember a letter my father wrote me. He always had the finest penmanship—perfect cursive writing. I received the letter in the mail a week before he passed away. And he reminded me of something in that letter that I, admittedly, have not always followed. In the letter, he wrote, "Bruce, remember what's important in life: your family and your loved ones and what they think of you." He went on to ask me, if I died tomorrow, who would show up at my funeral and what would they say? He said that money comes and goes and that I shouldn't let it define me. Relationships are the most important. There were a lot of years when I didn't think that way; I believed I needed to chase money as the most important thing. In recent years, I have come to realize that I want to leave a legacy. I want to help people become better humans, better versions of themselves. Grow your business *and* bring value to others. Be remembered for something more than making money.

It's true that when you have a purpose, just having money is not enough. Money provides for a lot in our lives, and it can bring temporary happiness, but at the end of the day, it's really nothing more than a facilitator. Sadly, I've worked with many people who have suffered from depression who are worth $20, $30, $50, or even $100 million. They have money but no purpose. Some people inherit money and build a company solely to generate more wealth. And then sometimes they sell their company to make even more money. So now they're 100 million dollars richer, but they don't have a purpose. They're not really serving people or changing lives. Having a product that does well and makes a lot of money doesn't mean that you are leading from a place of serving others.

My father understood something that took me years to learn: money without purpose is a hollow victory. This lesson became painfully clear as my business grew and I began working with clients who had achieved everything our culture defines as success. Deep down, though, some of them were struggling with something deeper. I've known three people who have committed suicide. They were clients of mine, and I knew them and their families very well. And I couldn't understand why this happened. The best conclusion I came to was that none of them had a purpose. They loved their families and worked hard to build their companies, but deep down, they hadn't defined their purpose—the thing that drove them to keep going.

I'm reminded time and time again how right my father was about not making money the priority. Little did I know all the ways that I would find fulfillment in different professions over the years or that I would find my purpose in my boyhood dreams. I honestly believe you can't have pleasure without purpose because pleasure is short-lived if not accompanied by a greater goal. I will forgo some pleasures to prioritize my purpose. It's the best feeling in the world to have a purpose-driven mission.

What purpose do you have? What mission are you on? If you find your purpose, whether it's business, personal, or charitable work, make it your life's calling.

BUSINESS BITES

- **Let your passions drive your purpose. Building your business around your interests keeps you motivated.** Who did you look up to as a kid? What did you daydream about becoming when you grew up? Those early influences and dreams can provide clarity for your interests now. When your business aligns with your interests, your motivation to succeed is that much greater. Write a one- to two-sentence purpose statement that will help you stay focused, even when life throws you curveballs.
- **Embrace challenges. Growth requires seeking discomfort.** How can you find ways to get outside your comfort zone? Apply to speak at a conference in your area of expertise. Apply for a job that feels challenging. Reach out to your customers and gather honest feedback on your product or service. By leaving the familiar environment of my home in High Bridge for the Marine Corps, I gained opportunities that would never have happened had I stayed in my small hometown. Take risks and put yourself out there. Stepping out of your comfort zone and accepting tough challenges can help you find your true purpose.
- **Use your past setbacks as valuable data for future success.** Your past doesn't define you. Previous setbacks—whether academic struggles, failed ventures, or personal mistakes—

don't determine your potential and should not influence your future. What lessons did you learn from your past experiences, and how can you channel them into better decision-making moving forward? Examine what went wrong, and use what you learn to improve your processes.

- **Define your business's core values and live by them.** Core values are more than just a nice idea; they guide every decision you make in business and in life. What are your non-negotiables? What beliefs drive you to want to succeed? Write down three to five core values and let them guide you. Operating your business with clear values helps you stay the course when things get tough.

CHAPTER 2
DISCOVERING THE "WHY" THAT DRIVES YOU

I t wasn't until I started living out my purpose that I felt fulfilled in my life. Finding my "*why*" has helped me continue to live out my purpose. I've had four very special and unique opportunities in my professional life: the Marine Corps, working for the LAPD, my body-guard business, and Quest Nutrition. In each of these opportunities, I have been able to discover my three "whys" and how they drive every-thing that I do.

My first "why" is to do as much as you can for as many people as you can and expect nothing in return. Doing this has brought me more opportunities and opened more doors than I could ever count. Providing value to others is a fundamental skill I've learned through my own interactions, and it's something I like to teach to other people. With a little practice, it's not hard, and yet some people are resistant to doing it. It's easy to be selfish, but it's more fulfilling to be generous.

When I honorably exited the Marine Corps, I found myself in Southern California, pursuing my childhood dream of becoming a police officer. Interestingly, the priest I spoke to that day in my home-town years before was right. I didn't go back to High Bridge, New Jersey; I eventually joined the Los Angeles Police Department, which is considered to be one of the most prestigious police departments in the world. But let's take a step back.

When I first started the process to become a police officer, I applied to fifteen different police departments. This was before online applications, so I had to call each department and ask them to mail me an application. In the meantime, I was working two jobs: as a trainer at Gold's Gym in the evenings and as a part-time truck driver for my then father-in-law. I also had a newborn baby, and I needed more income. One day, I saw a job posting in the newspaper for a car salesman at a new Mitsubishi dealership. I thought, *Why not?* Better than working multiple jobs and being exhausted all the time. I took a chance and went down to the dealership to speak with the owner, Mike Graber. I told him that I would love to sell cars for him, and he asked me if I had any experience. I admitted that I didn't. But I had just been released from the Marine Corps, and I was in good shape, had a clean haircut, and looked respectable. He decided to take a chance on me.

I walked straight from that interview to the floor, and I started selling cars that same afternoon. For the next year, while I was going through the process of becoming a police officer, I was the number one car salesman at that dealership. I figured out that it wasn't just about selling cars; the key was people skills. To be honest, I didn't know all that much about cars. I knew the basics about all of the models, but the connection I made with the customer is what sold the car. I truly listened to what the customer wanted and needed. Not only did I become the number one car salesman, but I would also get referrals. I would sell a car to someone, and next thing you know, the following day or weekend, someone would come in and say, "Hey, I was told to come in and ask for you." This happened because I created truly authentic relationships with my customers. No ulterior motives. No forcing people. Just a genuine connection.

When customers gave me their word that they would come back, I would let them leave. Some of the senior sales guys would get upset with me over this because it's unacceptable to let the customer leave the lot without another salesperson coming out to close the deal.

When I did this, it really upset some of the old-timers. Normally, no one *ever* comes back. In my experience, though, people *would* come back. Sometimes, I'd tell people, "Just go home and sleep on it. There's no pressure." As a car salesman, this was unheard of, and so I was a unique individual. And those people would come back after sleeping on it, ready to buy a car. They trusted me. I was honest with them, and I didn't push them. That's why I became the number one car salesman.

While I was applying to different police departments, Officer Williams with the LAPD was assigned to look into my background and contact my current and previous employers, as well as my friends, family, and neighbors. He was thorough, and he went to the Mitsubishi dealership on one of my days off to talk to the owner. I must have gotten a stellar review, because the next day, when I came in, Mr. Graber called me into his office and said, "I didn't know you wanted to be a police officer!"

I said, "Yes, sir, it's a boyhood dream of mine." I don't think he was trying to dissuade me when he said, "Let me present you with an opportunity, Bruce. There's something about you. Customers keep coming in asking for you, and the management just loves you. What if I told you that within a year, you'd be the manager of this dealership, probably making over $150,000? Would it sway you at all?"

Keep in mind, at the time, the salary for an entry-level police officer with the LAPD was about $50,000. Stunned, I said, "Gosh, Mr. Graber, that's such a gracious offer. But my calling is to be a police officer." I explained that it was my passion, and I wasn't even doing it for money. I just wanted to be a police officer.

He said, "Well, that offer will always stand. Even if you want to come and work on weekends, that offer will always be available. I hope it works out for you as a police officer, but you always have a home here." I'll never forget his supportive words and kindness.

That experience selling cars taught me that success comes from genuinely connecting with people and serving their needs. This is a lesson that would prove invaluable as I prepared to enter the police force, a profession built on serving and protecting the community.

My second "why" is providing service to contribute meaningfully to other people's well-being and safety. It gives me a sense of fulfillment to be a servant leader, and this mindset creates a powerful foundation for business because it shifts focus from self-serving goals to goals that solve problems for others. I'll talk more about servant leadership in the next chapter. For now, I want to share how this "why" resonated with joining the police force, which became a calling for me to protect and serve the residents of the great city of Los Angeles.

As part of the background check for my application to the LAPD Academy, I had to answer a forty-page questionnaire. Officer Williams interrogated me line by line, asking everything from "When's the last time you drank?" to "When's the last time you smoked weed?" to which I replied honestly, "Oh, never. I don't drink." and "Weed? I've never tried it." I remember his doubtful stare every time I answered a question. He clearly couldn't believe me. He said, "Listen, we're going to send you down for a polygraph. You will get eliminated immediately if you lie." I got nervous because I had never done a polygraph before. I wasn't lying, but still, it was an intimidating process.

Finally, on Christmas Eve, I received a phone call. It was Officer Williams, and he said, "Hey, Cardenas, do you still want to be a police officer?"

I said, "Yes, more than anything in the world, I want to be a police officer."

"Well, I'm giving you an early Christmas present," he replied. "Congratulations, you're going to be a police officer. Report to the LAPD Academy on January 11."

He let me know I would receive an official letter from the city with all the details, but he wanted to congratulate me himself. He said, "Bruce, you know, there's something I've noticed about you during this process. I investigate a lot of people. Your honesty and your integrity have really shone through. I'm not saying I was trying to catch you in a lie, but my job really is to screen out people who aren't qualified. And Bruce, congratulations, you are quite qualified."

That call made my Christmas. It was probably one of the greatest moments of my life. Some of the best news I've ever received from a great person. Officer Williams eventually became a captain, and we've maintained a good relationship over the years.

The LAPD police cars display their motto: "To Protect and to Serve." Working with the LAPD elevated my purpose and my "why" to a new level. We were serving and protecting over nine million people; it was a great responsibility, and I was honored to carry out my duties as an LAPD officer. I could hardly believe it. My calling was bigger than High Bridge, New Jersey. I knew this was going to be an important milestone in my life.

On a cold January day, I reported for training. I lined up with ninety of my fellow classmates in front of our drill instructor, Sandy Kimber, one of the first female instructors at the LAPD Academy. She scared me to death when she said, "Look to your left and look to your right. Not all of you will make it through this process. Some of you are going to fail out academically, and you will not be here on graduation day."

Immediately, my heart started pounding. My mind began spinning with anxiety as I thought to myself, *Here I am once again. I'm just the same guy who got held back in third grade, barely squeaked out of high school, and struggled to pass every test he has ever taken.* I was determined to do better in the police academy.

That same day, they issued our equipment, and then we got to know our classmates. I met James, who is a close friend to this day. We lived in the same area, so we carpooled together. On the hour-long commute, we took turns quizzing each other. We took notes in class on everything we learned so we could study together; we did this week in and week out, and on weekends, too.

When I got my first test back as a trainee in the LAPD Academy, it was a 92. That's not a C or a D—that's an A! The first test I'd ever passed with flying colors; I couldn't believe it. Reflecting on my younger years, I realized I had never applied myself in school. I wasn't dumb; I just wasn't interested. In the police academy, I enjoyed what I was learning, and I put in the effort to apply myself.

In the end, I was in the top 80 percent of my class academically. What I'm most proud of is graduating with top honors in self-defense, driving, tactics, physical ability, and firearms. It was one of the most fulfilling experiences in the world. I learned that I am smart and capable when I set my mind to something that I care about. I encourage you, if you find your calling and you're excited about it, don't worry about your past. Don't let it define you. Let your purpose and your "whys" arm you with the drive to succeed.

As a police officer, my annual salary was not tremendous, and I had a family to feed. I wanted to make extra money. I ran into a guy who was just retiring and owned a security company. I didn't know anything about the security business other than that I did security details in the Marine Corps. He said to me, "You know, you're a young, squared-away guy, and I could use some help." I started working for him and some very high-profile people on the Forbes list. You know, people who can be recognized by one name only, such as Arnold, Stallone, Cher, Madonna, Kim, and Paris.

This business opportunity further propelled my "why" of protecting people. I wanted to help people feel a sense of security and not worry about their surroundings. Two years into my career as a police officer, I decided to start my own security business. I knew nothing about being an entrepreneur. I just took the leap. I went through the process, got licensed and insured, and started my own company. I developed quite a successful bodyguard security business that was expanding not only nationally but also internationally. I had a great office and no complaints about where I was in life. I was about to discover that life had a surprise in store for me: a chance encounter at the gym that would reveal my third, unexpected "why."

At the age of forty-eight—proof that your "whys" can come later in life —I found my mission-based "why," which came from the fulfillment and satisfaction of changing people's lives during my time at Quest Nutrition. It started out as just a protein bar company to me, but it became so much more. Witnessing the impact of the product on people's lives transformed the work I was doing into something very meaningful. When you can see and measure how your business genuinely transforms lives, work becomes less about personal achievement and more about creating positive change in the world.

So, how did I get started with Quest Nutrition? Well, one day, I serendipitously met two amazing people in the gym, Shannan and Ron Penna. We became gym acquaintances, making small talk when we saw each other. About a month after meeting them at the gym and seeing them occasionally, I was at the Los Angeles Fitness Expo and came across a little booth where they were selling protein bars. These bars would one day become the first product of the brand Quest Nutrition, but this was long before that level of success. I reconnected with them, and Shannan gave me some bars to sample. I saw them maybe a couple of weeks later and told them that I thought the bars were amazing. She told me a little more about the company. She made the bars in a small handful of flavors in their kitchen, and Ron commercialized them. She gave off this magnetic energy when she was talking. I'd never seen someone so excited about a product.

What happened next was kind of a blur. I took a chance and asked if they wanted me to take some of the bars and get them into people's hands. I don't know why I offered because I'd never done anything like that before. I wasn't in the nutrition space; I was a bodyguard. Still, I felt compelled to help them essentially market their product for free. A few days later, Shannan dropped some product off at my house. It wasn't a lot because they were a tiny company, but it was enough.

I took the bars to a golf tournament where I was working as a bodyguard, and my friend Cheryl, the publicist, offered to get some people to give their reactions on camera. Mind you, this was 2012. Instagram was fairly new, and social media didn't exist the way it does today. Blogs were popular, but there weren't live videos or reels or any of the instantaneous sharing like you can do now. The host of the event created some content using the videos Cheryl took, and I showed them to Shannan and Ron. It was a hit, and they kept bringing me bars to share with people. I even brought some to Mario Lopez when I was doing security for him on the set of *Extra*.

Not long after, Ron invited me to visit their office in Paramount, which is south of L.A. They were in a not-so-great part of town, in an industrial strip mall with graffiti on the walls and broken-down cars in the parking lot. It didn't scream "success" from the outside. Inside, they had two small rooms with mini IKEA desks, like you might buy for your middle school kid. They had about eight people crammed into one of the rooms, working at these tiny desks, trying to get this thing off the ground.

What I saw was passion and desire and a sense of fulfillment. I fell in love with their process. They were on a mission to help people, and I wanted to help people, too. I felt like I was a part of that mission when I was sharing the product with people. We also started getting feedback on the product, which really solidified that we were doing something important. People started writing blog posts and emails, saying:

I lost thirty pounds over the last four months, and you changed my life.

I have diabetes, and my blood sugar doesn't spike when I eat these bars.

I have celiac disease, and I'm able to eat your bars.

I had gastric bypass surgery, and I can digest the bars. My doctor said I can chop them up into smaller portions to eat them.

When that started happening, I realized they were doing way more than just making protein bars; they were saving lives. It was like a light bulb went off. I knew I wanted to continue working with this company in some capacity. People saw these bars as a healthy alternative to eating candy or some other junk food. We started changing what the food supply chain looked like and shifting people's perspective on food. I became obsessed with getting the products out into different communities and into the right people's hands. I wanted to change people's lives.

I went to my first Celiac convention; I didn't even know such a thing existed. But when we learned about it, we knew we needed to be there. At the event, people from all walks of life gathered, some obese, some thin; they were all just glad to finally find something they could eat. When you look people in the eye as they express their gratitude for making a product they can safely eat, it stirs an indescribable emotion inside. I knew we needed to do more, to help more people. That really solidified my "why."

We did another event with the gastric bypass community. I kept meeting people who would tell me, "Your company saved my life. I have a go-to snack, and it doesn't affect my medical conditions." Obviously, obesity is rampant in this country; I felt like we made an impact in that area. It was very meaningful to see the effects of this product on people's health and nutrition.

I'm grateful to have discovered these three "whys" over the course of my career. I have been incredibly lucky and blessed by the opportunities that helped solidify them. Obviously, my three kids are also a big "why" in my life. I haven't been focused only on business; family is important to me, too. But we're here to talk about business.

I want you to know: if you haven't found your reason yet, your "why," it's never too late. Remember that I was forty-eight when I met the founders of Quest Nutrition in the gym. My life trajectory was more or less set; I ran a successful security business. And then, boom, all of a sudden, I was in the nutrition space. I'm probably the least qualified person on paper to work in a nutrition company, but I put myself out there. I took a risk, and it became a "why" for me.

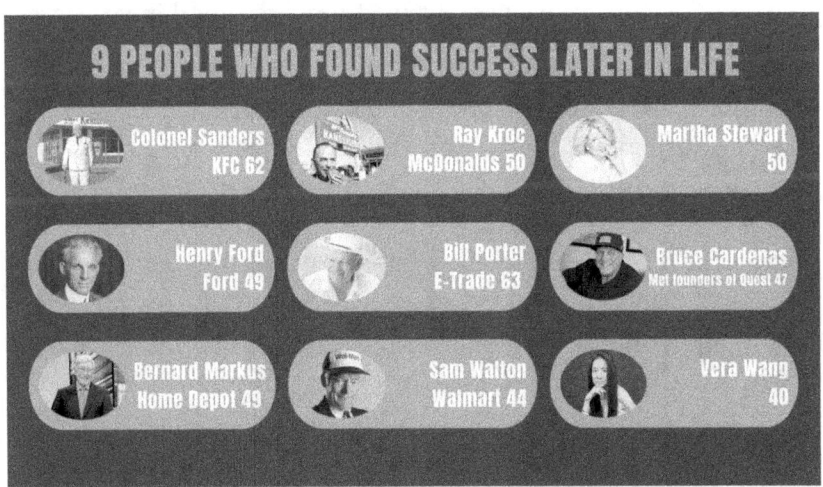

If I had walked in off the street and handed my resume to the receptionist, I probably wouldn't have even gotten an interview. What were my qualifications? I had experience as a bodyguard and a cop. It was my passion for their product and my interest in helping them without expecting anything in return that got me a foot in the door. I made a commitment to help them grow their brand because I believed in it, and that's how I solidified my future with the company.

It's never too late to find your why. And it's never too late to pursue your dreams. Sometimes people think, *I'm too old*, or *I've been doing this for twenty years; I can't do anything else.* It's never too late to switch careers. I think a lot of people have regrets at the end of their lives, disappointed that they never found their why or their purpose. I'm telling you, from personal experience, it's never too late. Take a risk on something you care about.

Finding your "why" may not be an easy path. It may be an obstacle course. There may be some hurdles. Do whatever it takes to find yours —it is worth it. My advice is to think of the three most impactful connections or relationships in your life and consider whether any of them can guide you to your "why." Can they help you explore your purpose? Can you find the drive within to discover where your true fulfillment lies? Lean on people that you trust, and ask for direction. It's okay to ask for help! If you're bringing value, people will want to help you. Your "why" may even come from a relationship you haven't found yet.

Bring value to as many people as you can with no expectations of anything in return. Opportunities will come, doors will open, and you'll find yourself in rooms you never thought possible. I'm the perfect example of that. I've visited the White House five times as a bodyguard. But I belong in the rooms I have been in. I didn't always think that, being a dumb kid from New Jersey, a C/D student. Now I look for opportunities to make myself a better person and to fulfill my "whys." I'm the real deal. I live by my purpose and my why every day.

If you haven't found it yet, your "why" is out there. Don't wait for the perfect moment to find it, though. My journey with Quest Nutrition began with a simple offer to help share protein bars; I didn't have some big vision to change lives, not at the beginning. Let your "why" reveal itself through action, not perfection or contemplation. Take small steps toward what interests you, bring value wherever you can, and stay open to where those steps might lead.

BUSINESS BITES

Get a journal or pull out some sticky notes and reflect on the recommendations and questions below. Use your answers to guide your actions moving forward in your business.

- **Your "why" is your competitive advantage—find it and live it.** Most entrepreneurs chase money first and wonder why they burn out when things get tough. Your "why" fuels your purpose and keeps you fired up to put in the work. Define your "whys." Write them on a sticky note and put them somewhere you can see them every day. Revisit them monthly. When making decisions about your business, ask yourself, *Does this opportunity align with my "why" and my purpose?* If not, walk away.
- **Provide value without expectations, and you'll open unexpected doors.** I'm not talking about being a pushover or giving your services away indefinitely. I'm talking about leading with value to create opportunities you can't plan for. Find regular opportunities each month to provide value to a cause that you believe in—perhaps it's a nonprofit, a company you admire, or a person you meet at a coffee shop with a cool business idea. Look for these moments in your daily interactions. Don't give your time to just anyone, though. The key is choosing wisely, not helping blindly.
- **Your "why" can emerge at any stage of life. Don't give up.** Age is not a limitation. Whether you're a twenty-something or have a few decades of work under your belt, you have unique experiences and perspectives. It's never too late to find deeper meaning in your work. Do you have an idea for a side

hustle? Who in your inner and outer circles is doing work that interests or inspires you? Is there an activity you gravitate toward? A problem you're itching to solve? If you're feeling stuck, ask yourself these questions, and your "why" will naturally follow.

- **Take action to discover your "why." Don't get caught in analysis paralysis.** The most important thing is to *do*. Set weekly goals for yourself based on your interests and inspirations, and *do them*. Take small steps toward what interests you. Sign up for a class where you can practice a new skill. Attend a networking event where you can meet new people. Don't wait for perfect clarity or perfect timing—there is no such thing. Let your "why" emerge through doing, not thinking or planning, without taking action.

*United States Marine Corp
graduation day*

*The LAPD—a boyhood
dream come true*

*With LAPD Chief Darryl
Gates, accepting the Police
Medal for Bravery*

Working with the LAPD Recruitment Division at the Miramar Airshow

*Proud to still be
a reserve officer
with the LA
County Sheriffs
after 30 years of
service*

*LAPD charity golf
tournament*

The 1992 Los Angeles Riots

*Chuck Norris
receiving his star on
the Hollywood Walk
of Fame*

CHAPTER 3
LEADING BY SERVING OTHERS

One summer, when I was sixteen, my dad asked me to help him with some work on a construction job. He offered to pay me cash at the end of the day. That made it pretty enticing, and I agreed. When we got to the job site, he assigned me some laborious tasks that took me about an hour and a half.

When I finished, I walked around the corner and saw my dad digging a ditch. There were other guys working on the construction site, moving and lifting materials and doing other odd jobs. I stood there for a minute staring at my dad. I asked him, "Hey, why are you digging a ditch? You own the company." He looked up at me from about two feet down into the ditch. He said, "You know what? You are so right, son. Please have this done by lunchtime," and handed me the shovel. He wanted me to dig up to the edge of the building wall, about twenty-five feet long, two feet deep, and eighteen inches wide. It's best not to repeat what my teenage self muttered under my breath, but I was seriously questioning how the hell the owner's own son got stuck digging this ditch.

At the end of the day, when I got in the truck with him to head back home, he said, "Listen. I know you're upset that I had you dig that ditch. Do you know why I was digging it myself? I own the company, and I have to lead by example. How can I ask someone else to dig a ditch if I can't show them how to do it? And we were short-handed. I could have easily waited for someone to finish another task and have them do it, but that would have delayed the workday. The work has to get done, and as the boss, sometimes you have to roll up your sleeves and do it yourself." Of course, at sixteen, I only cared about getting my cash at the end of the day, and I didn't fully comprehend the importance of what he told me.

I learned a similar lesson the next summer when my uncle invited me to come help him out at his landscaping business and nursery in Florida. I didn't really want to go, but at seventeen, I also didn't want to be at home with my parents all the time. When I was working with him, I witnessed him on many occasions digging ditches and doing manual labor. A year older and (a little) wiser, I really started to understand the importance of leading by example. Even though he did the same things my dad did, I had a different kind of admiration for my uncle. I remember coming home and telling my parents all about Uncle Ed digging ditches and doing the same work his workers did. My dad and uncle consistently demonstrated that real leadership means getting in the trenches with your team when necessary. They were servant leaders.

Providing value and having no expectations of receiving something in return is what servant leadership means to me. My dad and uncle demonstrated this by supporting their employees, putting in the work, and showing them what needs to be done. Putting others first and bringing value to your interactions goes a long way. To put it into an analogy, I always make more deposits than withdrawals in my day-to-day interactions. There's not a single person in my life who, if I called them to ask for a favor, would say, "Oh, gosh, Bruce, you've never done anything for me." I do things for other people out of a genuine desire to be helpful. Maybe that's one of my business languages: giving back to others. It's something I've always practiced, and it's come back to me tenfold, even though I never expect anything in return.

I understand that business owners need to take responsibility and do many tasks that they don't really want to do and that they may not get thanked for. I don't give a second thought when the trash needs to be emptied, for example. I don't look around and wait for a custodian. If I see that the trash needs to be emptied, I do it myself. Servant leadership is second nature to me.

This approach might seem obvious, but over the years, I have learned that many leaders struggle with this basic principle. I traveled forty weekends a year when we were building Quest Nutrition, and I met a lot of people—CEOs, visionaries, and entrepreneurs. I observed their behaviors and how they treated other people. A lot of those people fell short of being servant leaders. I think too many people become complacent, feeling that it's "not their responsibility" to do menial work that isn't in their job description or that they think doesn't apply to them as business owners. The reality is that it's everyone's responsibility to lead by example. It's simply the responsible thing to do. When it comes to owning a business and getting things done, there is no title, hierarchy, or ego worth getting in the way.

Whether you're the CEO or working in an entry-level position, you can take charge and act as a servant leader. Just because something isn't in your job description doesn't mean you can't go outside the box and help in other departments, leading by example. Every company needs that kind of spirit. Every entrepreneur needs those kinds of people on their team. I was coined an "intrapreneur" at Quest Nutrition because I created my own destiny. I saw gaps, and I filled them. I took the actions I felt were necessary to grow the brand. I had no job description when I first started at Quest Nutrition; I just had a strong desire to serve others. I remember Ron said to me, "This is a blank slate. We are just starting the company; anywhere you think you can bring value, just jump in." He explained, as a generalization, that the bigger a company gets and the more employees it hires, the more problems it faces. He needed help, and I wanted to give it.

For nine months, I attended events and conferences. I built Quest Nutrition's presence at fitness expos, focusing on getting the products into the hands of both everyday people and celebrities. There would be a local fitness event, and I would register and pay with my own credit card. I would secure a table and a tablecloth and get boxes of bars to display. Then I would attend the event by myself and talk to people about the product, handing out free samples. I never expensed the fees or my time. I became an expert on the product, and soon, Ron was asking others to send me opportunities we could get involved with. My goal was to bring value, and I didn't expect anything in return. And that's what I did.

Ron eventually learned that I was paying for everything related to these events at my own expense. He pulled me aside one day and commended me for my initiative, but told me to start expensing everything. I had no problem paying because I knew these events were important to the business, so I just took care of the cost myself. I wasn't looking for accolades. Shortly after that conversation, Ron took me to lunch. He said, "Bruce, you're an ambitious person. You've done so much great work for us, often without even being asked or told what to do. You are bringing us a lot of value, and we're basically stealing from you. We want to start paying you."

I mentioned the free protein bars they were giving me, and I think Ron laughed. He told me, "You're worth more than protein bars. Starting Friday, you're on the payroll. Keep your day job; we're not paying you to come into the office. Keep doing what you do in the outside world to promote the product. Keep being who you are because you're making magic out there."

When I got my first paycheck, things felt more real. Now that they were paying me, I knew I needed to up my game and prove myself. That mentality was self-induced, coming from the pride I've mentioned in being a servant leader. I split my days between my bodyguard business and Quest Nutrition. I became obsessed with the company and what I could do to contribute to its success. At this juncture in Quest Nutrition's growth, it was impossible for us to say that it was definitely going to be a huge success. They were only selling protein bars. It wasn't like I bought into a journey where I knew for sure I was going to make out rich. I received a decent paycheck every month, but there was no guarantee of future success or a full-time job. There were no false or misleading conversations with the leadership at Quest Nutrition. They never said, "You're going to get rich with us."

They gave me an opportunity, and I took my vision and my obsession with customer service, and I ran with it.

Servant leadership is not about being in control. It's about empowering others to take control of their destiny. That's how Ron and the team were with me. They had problems, and I helped solve them. I also saw opportunities and ran with them. I built out their brand ambassador and athlete program, which was a sponsorship opportunity for athletes and influencers to promote the brand. I did demos at events and built retail partnerships with stores such as GNC and The Vitamin Shoppe. I attended charity events that our partners supported. I did what no one else was willing or wanted to do. Not everyone put in the same level of commitment to reach our goals. I didn't go to anyone and tell them what I was doing or ask for their permission. I saw what needed to be done, took charge, and made it happen. I felt empowered to take control of my own destiny.

Many people can't even fathom what that means. They're getting paid to do a job as a copywriter or a marketing director or whatever it is, and they don't want to put in extra work. They don't want to take charge; they just want to do the bare minimum. I always remind people that endless opportunities will come your way if only you act on them. Of course, you have bills to pay, and your 9-5 paycheck allows you to have a roof over your head and put meals on your table. But if there's an event at your company or a big deadline coming up, you can find out what you can do to contribute to the company's success. You can even take the initiative and think of something on your own. That's bringing value with no expectations, right?

Servant leadership doesn't only apply to CEOs or business owners. This mindset works at every level. Whether you work in real estate, finance, or marketing, what can you do to make your department or company better? How can you become an intrapreneur inside the company where you already work? Instead of asking what your company can do for you, find out what you can do without being asked, and do it.

Don't think for a minute that people won't recognize your efforts. And don't let the naysayers get you down. There will be people who call you a suck-up or who are resentful that you're lending a helping hand. At the end of the day, it's your journey and your success. So, if you can bring value to the circle you're in, no matter what it is, bring it. Don't worry about what other people think.

My experiences taught me that servant leadership isn't about grand gestures—it's visible in the daily choice between waiting for someone else to handle a problem or stepping up yourself. When you see a colleague who needs help or a gap that no one else is filling, you face that same choice my father gave me: complain about the ditch, or pick up the shovel.

Reflect for a minute on your role as a servant leader. The answer becomes clear when you honestly examine your default response to problems. Do you instinctively look for someone else to handle it, or do you ask what you can contribute? Your pattern of behavior over time—not your intentions—reveals whether you're truly leading through service or just talking about it.

When you want people to invest in your company—and I mean emotionally and with energy as an employee—you have to think about what you're doing to invest in them. You might say, "Well, the employees get paid." And yes, pay is important, and most people need a paycheck to live and support their families. But many employees say they would sacrifice a raise to be in a culture of respect and dignity at work.

Culture is a word that I think people don't fully understand. You can't wave a wand and, boom, suddenly you have a great company culture. It takes work. And it's not the kind of work most people think it is. It's not about having a game room, offering great snacks, or buying a fancy espresso machine. That's not culture. Culture is about how you treat people—from top-level management to entry-level employees. People are often pigeonholed in their job, in their cubicle, just expected to do the work and grind every day. It's important to embrace every single employee as part of the larger team and to acknowledge and support their contributions to the company. That's what a servant leader does.

The numbers speak for themselves. Studies show that companies with a strong team-oriented culture are twenty-one percent more profitable than their competitors (Gallup).[1] Organizations that prioritize collaboration see five times higher employee retention rates and generate thirty percent higher innovation levels (Forbes).[2] These statistics reflect the power of collective effort—when individuals work together, they create a synergy that far exceeds the sum of their parts.

A great culture is born from the values you bring to your employees and how much you appreciate them for the work they do to help the company accomplish its goals. It's about listening to your employees— really, truly listening—and proving to them that their opinions matter by taking action and trusting them to take initiative in the company. It's about putting your employees first. When you truly have a culture that is in sync, people want to do their best work. They want to go above and beyond to perform well and explore ways to enhance the company's growth and success.

A friend of mine recently asked me to come by his office for the day. He thought his company had a great culture, but he also felt something was missing and wanted my advice. So, I spent the day with him, and at the end of the day, I had some questions. I asked him, "When was the last time you went and sat with your employees and talked to them?" He told me that wasn't his job—he has managers for that reason. But my friend had fifty total employees at his company. There was no reason that he shouldn't know all of their names (which he didn't). He told me he was very proud of his employees, but I'm pretty sure they didn't know that. He claimed to have an open-door policy. But he had a gatekeeper—a receptionist—who sat outside his

1. Harter, Jim. "Employee Engagement on the Rise in the U.S." Gallup.com, April 23, 2025. https://news.gallup.com/poll/241649/employee-engagement-rise.aspx.
2. Kate Vitasek, "The Power of Collaborating With Employees for Innovation," *Forbes*, January 13, 2025, https://www.forbes.com/sites/katevitasek/2025/01/13/the-power-of-collaborating-with-employees-for-innovation/.

door. And when I was there, I watched her constantly stop people from entering the CEO's office and interrogate them about what they needed.

That's not creating a positive culture; it's creating a divide. He was so disconnected from his employees that he had no idea how they felt about working for him. So I gave him some advice. I advised him to step out of his CEO office at least once a week and talk to his employees. To go sit in the common areas, sit with different departments, and ask people their names. Find what they do, as well as their dreams and desires, both professional and personal. Determine whether the culture he is building is one they are embracing or if they think anything critical is missing. Ask people to be honest and transparent with him. Show them that he cares about them and wants them to be happy and to succeed.

It's easier said than done. Many employees will not be honest or transparent for fear of retribution. You may have to do an anonymous survey. We had to do this at Quest Nutrition. Early on at the company, everyone was committed to the mission: helping people stay healthy, lose weight, and have snacks that fit a variety of dietary restrictions. We grew quickly, and it was exciting. Then, at one point, there was a rift, and suddenly, everyone wasn't aligned on the company culture and vision. One person started to see things differently and wanted to take the company in a direction that didn't match our trajectory at the time or the goals of most of the leadership team. On top of that, employees complained they couldn't access certain leaders. So, Ron and the team conducted an anonymous survey.

The results were concerning. People felt there was a disconnect between executive leadership and everyone else. Three of the top people in the company were rated as unapproachable, egotistical, and narcissistic. Many employees reported that they did not bring any value to the company. This is not the kind of feedback you want about your leadership team. The survey opened our eyes to the fact that certain individuals were not aligned with the vision and culture we had created. Some people were no longer on the same journey as the owners. They lost sight of our mission and became more self-serving.

Without that survey, we never would have known. We thought we had developed this amazing culture, but people were afraid to share their feelings directly with certain leaders.

There are two kinds of companies. There's the kind of place where you want to show up every day and give your all. The kind of place where you don't miserably watch the clock, where you feel valued and appreciated. The kind of company where you're not micromanaged. And then there's the kind of company where you feel like people are watching you, looking over your shoulder, questioning every move you make. The kind of place where you want to clock out as soon as your shift or obligation is over. Your calendar is full of frivolous, pointless meetings, and the higher-ups control everyone's creativity.

With the first kind of company, it can be taken one step further to implement something known as decentralized command, a term popularized by former Navy SEAL Jocko Willink. In business, this concept is known as a flat hierarchy. The idea is that everyone is equal. Everyone at the company can lead because they each bring unique expertise and experience to the table. No one questions what they do, and when their knowledge is needed, they are engaged by their peers and higher-ups to contribute. That might mean taking the lead on a project or a mission. There's a dynamic understanding among all team members, and even people who technically outrank them on paper respect and understand their expertise and their ability to get the job done. There is likely still a CEO and higher-level executives, but they realize the company's success depends on people's independence and freedom to think and act in full autonomy.

Ron Penna embodies this type of leadership. Having worked closely with him at two companies now, he reminds me all the time that he doesn't want to make decisions. He wants to be told what to do and what is happening. Others often laugh it off and say that he's just kidding, but I can assure you that he's not. He's serious; he doesn't want to make decisions. Essentially, no one is "in charge." Everyone does their job, everyone excels, and everyone brings value to the table. He wants his employees to come to him to tell him how they're approaching a problem. They might come to him looking for validation, but they're smart, and they already have the solution. So, he often puts the validation back on the rest of us: what do *we* think is the best answer? In turn, we're empowered to make decisions and move forward with them.

At Legendary Foods, we sometimes struggle because new hires often come from corporate environments and aren't used to a flat hierarchy. They immediately think there's a chain of command or a corporate structure. Even though we've conveyed to them that this is how we work, they are still in the habit of immediately going to someone of higher authority in the company to get the validation they think they need to move forward with a project. This causes delays, red tape, and unnecessary bureaucracy. Over time, they get more comfortable and learn to trust their instincts.

A flat hierarchy makes for a happier, more productive workplace. Your employees are the backbone of your business. There has to be strong communication, relationships of trust, and advocacy for your employees to be their best. My advice is to talk to your employees. Get to know them. Build a true open-door policy, and they are likely to be honest and share their feelings and ideas. If you think something is off with your culture, send out an anonymous survey. You will get even more honesty that way.

And if you want to have a successful entrepreneurial journey and eventually exit your company by selling it for a tremendous amount of money, remember that not just any company can do this. When an investment firm considers helping to sell a company, someone from the firm spends time there. They want to know who the leaders are, who the workers are, if they're happy, and if they think the company is being managed well. If you have unhappy people who do not buy into the culture and who don't feel supported, you'll likely face disappointment when it comes time to reap the rewards of your success.

As a servant leader, you should always aim to prioritize the needs of others, especially your team or community, over personal ambition or authority. Servant leadership requires humility, a genuine desire to empower others, and a focus on long-term growth and well-being. The ultimate goal of a servant leader is to create an environment where people can thrive and contribute meaningfully to shared goals.

BUSINESS BITES

- **Build leadership credibility by putting in the work.** When you're a business owner, you can't ask others to handle tasks you're unwilling to do. Make a list of areas in your business where you need to step in and do the work to model for your team. Leading by example builds respect and trust with your team. The daily choice between stepping up or waiting for someone else to act shows whether you're genuinely committed to serving others or just talking about it.
- **Go beyond your job description to build leadership skills.** Whether you're a business owner or an employee at someone else's company, you can identify gaps and fill them without being asked. Is there a process that could use updating? Is there an event that needs to be staffed? Don't wait for someone else to handle problems that you see arise. Take that opportunity to offer your skills or learn something new. Sticking rigidly to defined roles won't help you grow.
- **Invest your own resources when you believe in something.** I'm not telling you to spend money you don't have. Think about how you can contribute to a cause that's important to you. Can you donate items to an event you're working on? Can you give a few hours on evenings or weekends to promote a product or service or a nonprofit that you care about? Putting a little extra skin in the game proves your dedication and can open doors to new and exciting opportunities.
- **Provide value without expecting recognition.** While recognition is nice, it shouldn't be your primary motivator. And you shouldn't assume you'll get immediate accolades for the extra effort you put in. Focus on contributing meaningfully, and opportunities will emerge from the value you provide consistently over time.

- **Embrace the concept of a decentralized command/flat hierarchy.** If you're a manager or business owner, reflect on how you can empower your team to make decisions independently. What would happen if you let your employees take charge within their areas of expertise? The result might surprise you, in a good way. If you are an employee in a traditional 9-5 corporate setting, you can start by making small decisions within your scope of work without seeking unnecessary approval. Present solutions to problems with confidence, instead of as a question. In all business settings, it's possible to embody this concept.

Guest appearance on NFL on Fox with Rehan Jalali, Howie Long, Tony Gonzalez, and Michael Strahan

Quest Nutrition at the Arnold World's Strongest Man competition with Sofia Vergara

Quest Nutrition taking over New York at the NY Pro Bodybuilding Championships

Representing Quest at the Nickelodeon Kids' Choice Awards

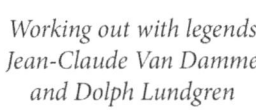

Working out with legends Jean-Claude Van Damme and Dolph Lundgren

CHAPTER 4
MASTERING THE ART OF CONNECTION

I t was my first day on the job with the LAPD. I met Bob during roll call as he was assigned as my first training officer. Bob told me to grab all my equipment and meet him at the car. I was more ready than ever to finally get started fulfilling my dream of being a police officer. I got into the passenger seat and set everything up. I put a notepad on the armrest between us; that was how we jotted down notes if we needed to identify someone or remember details during a radio call.

Bob picked up the notepad and drew a picture of a face—a big circle with two big eyes and two big ears. No mouth. And he said, "Bruce, this is you. I need you to do a lot of looking and listening, and no talking. Are we clear?"

I responded, "Yes, sir," as dutifully as I could.

Now, keep in mind, I was twenty-five years old and fresh out of the Marine Corps. I was jacked and confident, and I felt like this guy was talking to me like I was a child. But I sucked it up and listened. Bob then said, "Listen with the intent to understand. That's what's going to keep you and me alive. You see, Bruce, the more you watch and listen, the greater your chances are of capturing information in the real world. People listen, but they don't usually listen to understand. They listen to reply. And sometimes they don't even let you complete your thoughts. They're already replying without even listening."

I never got to tell Bob that he taught me one of the most important skills I have ever learned. Of course, at the time, I didn't realize how important this skill would be throughout my career. I do not exaggerate when I say that this is a skill I use almost more than any other, in both my personal and professional life. And Bob was right. I encounter people every day in the business world who start replying before the other person has even finished talking. I've seen it happen to others, and it's happened to me hundreds of times.

There are three kinds of people: those who listen with the intent to understand, those who listen with the intent to reply, and those who don't listen at all. You'll know the last type of person because they won't even let you finish a sentence. Your goal is to fall into the first category.

How can you be listening if you're talking over someone? Or if you're preparing a response in your head while the other person is talking? If you're not actively listening, you're going to miss some important details in conversations. And you're going to miss a chance to learn about the other person. If you take the time to listen, to focus on what the other person is saying before you reply, you'll be able to fully take in what they're saying to you. You'll be listening with the intent to understand. That's the key.

The smartest people are not always the ones talking. When you take the time to be fully engaged with your eyes and your ears, you'll be able to contribute something meaningful with your words. I have had a lot of practice putting this communication skill to good use over the years.

During my time as a bodyguard in security and transportation, my company was invited to an annual retreat hosted by NetJets, a private jet company owned by Warren Buffett. We owned a fractional share of a jet for transporting our clients. We had the smallest possible share, but we were eligible to attend the poker tournament the next day. Personally, I was the poorest person in the room by far as a bodyguard. This was a room full of some of the wealthiest people in the world.

Annual NetJets Poker Tournament at the Wynn Las Vegas with NetJets owner Warren Buffett, 2009.

The event was held at Wynn Las Vegas, a five-star hotel and casino. On the first morning, a breakfast buffet was served in one of the ballrooms. I filled up a plate and saw a gentleman sitting at a mostly empty round table. I asked to join him. Within a short period of time, the ten-person tables started to fill up. Lo and behold, here comes Warren Buffett, holding a cup of coffee and a Danish, asking if he could join us. Of course, we all said yes.

He sat right across from me, and people immediately started barraging him with questions, opinions, and business inquiries. Mind you, this was a poker tournament for all the jet owners. It was meant to be a relaxing and fun weekend, not a business conference of any kind. I could tell he was using his sense of humor to deflect people. His body language definitely said, "Hey, I'm just here to enjoy my Danish and my coffee and play some poker," but not everyone picked up on that. I watched people awkwardly continue to plug their businesses and self-proclaimed successes, shamelessly pontificating about themselves. Then something interesting happened.

Mr. Buffett, in the middle of all these people yapping at him, looked across the table at me, glanced at my name tag, and said, "Bruce, what brings you here?"

I replied, "Well, sir, I do security and transportation for some of the jet owners."

He said, "Well, shit, that sounds more important than anyone else in this room." He gave a small chuckle. I don't think anyone else at the table laughed; their attempts at bombarding Mr. Buffett to get his attention had been unsuccessful. He was having a conversation directly with me, and he even asked me to tell him more about my business. I explained the work that we do, then he asked me about myself—it was a simple conversation, lasting no more than a few minutes. Eventually, we all finished eating and left the table, and that was that.

Several hours later, the poker tournament started, and I was standing by the bar, next to two of the wealthiest men in the world. Mr. Buffett was nearby, and he turned to one of these men and said, "Oh, have you met my new friend Bruce? By the end of this weekend, I'm going to offer to buy his company, but he'll probably turn me down because he drives a hard bargain." We all laughed. That was his brand of humor.

Over the next two days, we acknowledged each other with a nod or a wave, and there was even a photo opportunity at one of the evening functions. When the weekend was over, the VP of Operations for NetJets came up to me and asked if I had spoken to Mr. Buffett. My initial thought was, *Oh my gosh. I'm in trouble.* But I said, "Yes, I talked to him a bit at breakfast and here and there during the tournament."

The VP said to me, "Well, he really liked you, and he wants to see what we can do to increase the amount of NetJets business that your company receives." I couldn't believe it! I replied, "That would be great; that's very generous of Mr. Buffett. I appreciate it."

The major takeaway here is that I listened. I listened to Mr. Buffett at the breakfast table, and I listened to those around him trying desperately to pitch their businesses and ideas. I didn't interject, I didn't override or interrupt anyone. I observed. I hung back. I was the only one who did that, and Mr. Buffett noticed that I wasn't acting like everyone else, trying to suck up to him. And when I did talk to him, I spoke maybe thirty words total. I didn't ramble on and on or try to make everything about me. I was kind and respectful. Honestly, I was humbled to be at the event. I wasn't a millionaire; I was a bodyguard. I think it's important to stay humble, no matter how rich, important, or famous you are. I had no intentions of getting something out of my conversations with Mr. Buffett.

The single greatest communication skill you will ever acquire is listening. More specifically: listening with the intent to understand what the other person is saying. In my interactions with Mr. Buffett, this skill proved to be invaluable.

I think it's important in every aspect of life to be a good communicator and a strong negotiator. Too many people jump to conclusions. Too many people don't listen. Too many people escalate a situation. I've worked with many people who lose all rational thought and start yelling and disrespecting others in the heat of the moment. I always try to stay calm and listen to understand people's needs. If you get worked up, you can't solve anything and will probably only make things worse. My time as a bodyguard, especially, helped me understand social cues. I knew how to read a room and could immediately spot the pecking order of any group of people associated with my clients. As an entrepreneur, I continue to need this communication skill.

We all want to be heard, and our impulses sometimes drive us to talk before thinking or talk without listening. Controlling the urge to speak is something many people struggle with. You have to be able to control your impulse to blurt out all your thoughts and ideas when others are speaking. Some are better than others at controlling their impulses. Mastering communication means recognizing that moment when you feel compelled to speak and asking yourself a simple question: Will my words add value to this conversation, or am I just trying to get attention? The difference between these two motivations often determines whether you'll be remembered as someone worth knowing or someone to avoid.

You want to bring value to every conversation you're part of, and often the best way to do that is by listening and observing. The world isn't black and white—something that I learned every day in my work as a police officer. In the police academy, we learned policies, procedures, rules, and regulations. The first day I stepped out into the field, it felt like I had pretty much thrown everything I had learned out the window. When I got in the field with Bob, he all but said, "Forget everything you learned in the Academy, Bruce, because now you're in the real world."

Bob's advice was solid, but he had almost thirty years on the job, and he had become a little jaded, to be honest with you. I saw moments of kindness from him, but also moments of anger and frustration. I remember this one day very distinctly. We arrested a gentleman for a $3,000 outstanding warrant. He was a white guy—a tatted-up biker type from the San Fernando Valley, which is a rough part of the Valley known for making and selling meth. We took him into the station, and I remember pretty aggressively pulling him out of the police car by his handcuffs.

A young lieutenant watched as I brought him in and pulled me aside. After I told him what he was in for, he said to me, "That's it? You were a little rough with him." He paused for a second. Then he asked, "You're working with Bob, aren't you?" I nodded.

He said, "Bob's a good cop, but he's not what he once was. He's gotten pretty cynical. But, Bruce, you're a young man. You've got great energy —there's something about you. People gravitate toward you, and you toward them. You're a people person, and I hate to see you going down this path that Bob is dragging you on. How do *you* feel about this job, and how do *you* think you should treat people? Think about that, and make your own decisions."

By this point, I was really listening. He said, "I'll leave you with this final thought: That gentleman you brought in is someone's uncle, brother, father, cousin. For all you know, he has an eight-year-old son who adores him. Can you imagine if his kid saw you treating him like that?"

I went home that day with my head kind of spinning. I did some self-reflection, and I remember thinking, *Who am I to treat anyone with anything other than respect and dignity?*

Looking back, I was emulating my mentor. I watched and learned how Bob conducted himself as my training officer, and I acted with the same gruff behavior. I'm grateful to the lieutenant for giving me a true understanding of how to interact and communicate with people on the job. That conversation changed my whole outlook on my work as a police officer from that day on.

After that, every time I knocked on a door, arrested someone, or pulled someone over, I thought about the guy I had brought into the station for the $3,000 warrant. Bringing empathy into my work at the LAPD really shed a different light, honestly, on how I conducted myself and how I taught other people to conduct themselves. Following the spirit of the law rather than the letter of the law served me in my communication with others.

This approach—combining listening with empathy—got put to the test when I was assigned to work in South Central LA. Most police encounters there are negative, but I quickly learned there are plenty of good, law-abiding citizens in that neighborhood, too. Some of them had been released from prison and had nowhere to go. We'd conduct field identifications, checking IDs and asking people what they were doing.

Some officers I worked with were disrespectful, making assumptions without listening. They treated the people they encountered with very little compassion or professionalism. I approached everyone with empathy, lending a listening ear, and I found that my communication style got me much further. I could always find something in common with anyone—conversation often turned to lifting weights because of my size. On several occasions, it led to push-up contests with guys on the street.

My partners would ask why I was "trying to relate to those losers." Every time, I'd tell them what that young lieutenant taught me: these people are someone's father, brother, or cousin. Maybe they made mistakes or got caught up in something bad, but they've served their time. Doesn't everyone deserve empathy and to be heard? They hadn't thought of it that way; no one had ever even suggested that they think of it that way. When they tried that approach, they had better outcomes with people on the street as well. It goes to show that a little empathy, genuine listening, and strong communication skills can carry you far in any line of work.

It's critical to listen and communicate effectively. I've been a police officer, a bodyguard, and a business person, and I've seen similar behavior from people in every job I've held. There are three sides to every story. There's my story, and there's the customer's story—and the truth probably lies somewhere in the middle. To be an effective communicator, you have to listen intently to all sides of the story so that you can understand the problem and communicate a solution.

Understanding body language and being able to read a room when interacting with people are important. Not everyone can do it. You see, as a police officer, you often have to de-escalate a situation, and you could be in deep trouble if you can't pick up on social cues. The same goes for business. Whether it's a domestic violence situation or a customer dispute, tempers can flare, and rational thinking sometimes goes out the window.

I once had to let go of a bodyguard who couldn't control his impulses around a celebrity client. One of the biggest female recording artists in the world was my client for many years, and I sent one of my body-guards on a trip to Mexico for her video shoot because I couldn't go. I briefed him very clearly on the details of the trip, and he said he felt prepared. I reminded him that our job is to follow the security proto-cols to keep her safe and not worry about anything else—what she's doing or how she's spending her time is not our business, as long as she remains safe.

After the week-long photo shoot ended, I found out from her manager that my guy stepped out of line. He told me that they wouldn't use any of my other guys moving forward. They were basically going to sever ties with my company unless I could personally make myself available for a job.

Here's what happened.

Every evening, the client, the manager, and the crew invited our agent to join them at dinner, and every evening, he politely declined. I have never joined a client for dinner, and I always instructed our body-guards to do the same. Our job is to be nearby, keeping a close eye on everything. Finally, on the last night of the trip, they asked him again, and he gave in and joined them. He proceeded to have a couple of glasses of wine and started chatting with our celebrity client because his wife is a big fan. In an instant, he took the relationship from busi-ness to personal. He shouldn't have been at their table, he shouldn't have been drinking, and he shouldn't have gotten comfortable with the client. He broke the cardinal rules of protection. How can you be proficient at your job as a bodyguard if you're drinking? If you're chat-ting instead of paying attention to the surroundings?

I was rather frustrated and upset, but I kept my composure as the manager told me this story. After the meeting, I called the agent, and we met up. I asked him to tell me about the trip—of course, he down-played everything. But he had committed a serious offense.

When people can't control themselves around successful individuals, they often cross professional boundaries, damaging relationships. This was one of the biggest learning opportunities for me that some people cannot control their impulses around others. My guy stopped doing what Bob taught me on day one—he stopped observing. If he'd been paying attention like he should have been, he would have realized that saying no to dinner five nights in a row was the job. But he got caught up in the moment and forgot why he was there.

I've seen it happen time and time again, both in my personal and professional life. That's what happened with Mr. Buffett, too. People think, *I have my thirty seconds to take this shot and say everything I want to say to this person*, and they don't stop to think about what they're saying or if the other person is even interested. They want to gain respect and dignity, but often end up losing them in the process.

If you're only thinking about yourself and not the other person, that's a mistake. What I've learned from being around celebrities and successful people is that their brains shut off when someone immedi-ately starts pitching them something. That's exactly what happened with Warren Buffett. He was surrounded by people trying to get his attention, so he decided to talk to the one person who wasn't bombarding him.

When famous and successful people are in a public space, they're getting nothing but praise and solicitation and opportunities thrown at them. It's exhausting. The successful people that I have worked with have all said to me at some point, "Bruce, you're so quiet. I can relax around you. I don't have to think or worry about you trying to sell me on something. Everyone else I encounter starts telling me about an idea or pitching some opportunity, and then I'm constantly fielding requests from different people wanting something from me. It causes me to just shut down mentally and emotionally. You're not like that."

So how do you handle it when you do have something important to say to someone successful? I've found there's a simple approach that actually works. Instead of blurting out your pitch, you say, "Mr. Buffett, it's a pleasure meeting you. Would it be okay if I sent my idea to your assistant for you to review?" In this scenario, you're respecting their time and their process.

Most people won't take that approach, especially if they can't control their impulses or if they're not listening with the intent to understand. But I'm telling you, it works every time. You're not taxing them with too much thinking, and you're also being respectful of the communication and their boundaries and the opportunities before you.

The next time you're in the presence of someone important or in the middle of a conversation, pay attention and take notes. Whenever you feel the urge to speak impulsively or chime in on a topic, pause to think first. Are you contributing meaningfully to the conversation or interrupting? Are you bringing value to the conversation, or are you distracting from the conversation? It only takes one second to decide whether to speak up or stay on the sidelines and listen. Listening can lead to saying something that enhances the conversation.

It's human nature to struggle with impulse control, so I know this may sound difficult. It's a muscle you have to strengthen. I promise that in the long run, it will come back around to your benefit tenfold. People will respect you more for saying nothing rather than opening your mouth without thinking.

Practicing these qualities can transform your relationships, communication, and business success. In a world where so many people rush to speak and pay little attention to those around them, being the person who listens, observes, and builds meaningful connections will set you apart and take you far in life.

BUSINESS BITES

- **Listen like your success depends on it because it does.** Remember to always listen with the intent to understand, not reply. What I learned from Bob and proved with Warren Buffett is that the person who listens always wins. Before you open your mouth in any conversation, ask yourself the same question I do: "Will this add value, or am I just trying to be heard?" Nine times out of ten, you'll learn more and make a better impression by keeping quiet and really focusing on what the other person is telling you.
- **Treat everyone with dignity, no matter who they are.** That lieutenant changed how I saw my job when he reminded me that everyone is someone's father, brother, or son. Whether you're dealing with a CEO or someone sitting on a street corner, a little empathy and genuine listening will get you further than aggression or assumptions ever will.
- **Control your impulses around successful people—restraint is what's impressive.** I've watched countless people blow opportunities because they couldn't help themselves. When you meet someone important, your instinct will be to pitch them or prove how smart you are. Don't. Be the one person in the room who isn't trying to sell them something, and watch how they gravitate toward you.
- **Read the room before you jump into any situation.** Whether I was working the streets in South Central or standing in a ballroom full of millionaires, I always observed

first. Look at the social dynamics, figure out what's really happening, and understand the situation before you contribute. Your words carry more weight when you know what you're walking into.

- **Respect people's time and energy.** Instead of cornering someone with your big idea, do what I recommend: Offer to send it through their assistant or follow up later. This approach has opened more doors for me than any elevator pitch ever could. People remember when you respect their boundaries, and they'll think of you when real opportunities arise.

Paris Hilton

Touring campuses across the United States with the Dalai Lama

Kim Kardashian at her Vera Wang wedding dress fitting

International in-store appearance with Mariah Carey for a major album release

Music awards night with Jennifer Lopez

One of many movie premieres with Mel Gibson

Sammy Davis Jr.

Jim Carrey and Lauren Holly at the world premiere of The Cable Guy (1996)

At the Emmy Awards with Calista Flockhart for Ally McBeal (1998)

Man's best friend has also provided a layer of protection for some of my high profile clients

John Travolta, Kelly Preston, Mia Kirshner, and Dustin Hoffman at the world premiere of Mad City (1997)

Tom Cruise and Nicole Kidman

When the Bodyguard meets the Bodyguard— at the premiere of The Bodyguard (1992) with Whitney Houston and Kevin Costner

Herb Ritts and Cindy Crawford at a movie premiere

Chris Rock, Rene Russo, and Joe Pesci at the premiere of Lethal Weapon 4 (1998)

At the Golden Globes with Courtney Love, who was nominated for an award for The People vs. Larry Flynt (1996)

Kevin Bacon and Kyra Sedgwick at a Hollywood movie premiere

Arnold Schwarzenegger and James Caan at one of Schwarzenegger's many movie premieres

Courtney Love, Jim Carrey, and Danny DeVito at the Man on the Moon premiere (1999)

Joe Pesci

The Baldwin brothers at a charity billiards tournament

NFL legend Howie Long on the set of Fox Sports

Visiting the White House, where Mariah Carey performed for President Bill Clinton during Police Week

Baseball legend Dave Winfield when Fox took over Yankee Stadium for a special event

Providing security on the set of KTLA Los Angeles local news

Provided protection during the 1998 World Series

Jack Kemp, former U.S. Secretary of Housing and Urban Development

Welsh singer Charlotte Church

50th birthday celebration with Muhammad Ali

The cast of Interview with the Vampire on the press tour (1994)

One of my longest clients in executive protection, Revlon, where we handle personal security for some of the top models

CHAPTER 5
DEVELOPING RELATIONSHIP CAPITAL

About fifteen years ago, my team and I were deep in preparations for bodyguard duties at the GRAMMYs. That event is like the Super Bowl for the security business. My company was doing security for music label executives and artists, as well as doing production at the event and some of the after-parties.

It was the morning of the GRAMMYs, and everyone slept in because they had parties the night before. I decided to go down to the venue to make sure everything was set up and ready to go; this was the biggest event of the year for the label I was working with. There were barricades in place, and paparazzi were already lined up so they had the best spots for the red carpet. There were already spectators milling around as well.

As I was checking on things, a young kid came up to me and said, "Excuse me, are you Bruce?" The other security guys pointed me out as the one in charge, and he asked if he could speak with me. I told him to give me a minute so I could finish inspecting the venue, making sure everything was set up and ready to go. On my way back out, I honestly didn't want to stop. I remember thinking, *How do I avoid this kid?* But I always try not to dismiss people, and he seemed nice enough and like he had a good energy about him.

So I stopped and asked what I could help him with. He said, "I have an idea, and I'd like to meet your boss tonight." My first reaction was that that definitely was not going to happen.

He told me his name and that he was from Minnesota. He said, "I've been here in Los Angeles for a month. I'm trying to get in with a music label, any music label, because I have this amazing idea. It's a technical thing. I have an answer to one of the music industry's problems."

I said, "That's pretty amazing, but I don't know how I can help you. I'm in the security business."

He knew who I worked with—the name of the music label and the CEO. He had seen me at a few other events and made the connection. He said to me, "I'm on my last dime. My mom wants me to come home. She thinks I'm chasing a dream that won't be fulfilled. I can't get in anywhere. I've knocked on every door, every label. No one will even take a meeting. I've tried to drop off my resume. I can't even get past a receptionist."

I thought for a second, and then I told him, "Look, I don't know if this will work or not, but why don't you try this? If you do ever get in front of anyone at a music label, tell them you have an idea, and you'll work for them for free."

His face dropped when I said this. I continued, "Just tell them, 'Whether it's two months or six months or a year, I'll work for you for free. And at the end of whatever period of time you deem appropriate, if you're happy with my service, please consider hiring me.'"

He seemed dejected. He told me he couldn't afford to do that. I replied, "I don't know what to tell you. If you really want to get in with a music label, go get a shift at Starbucks starting at 5 a.m. so you can be finished by 9 a.m. Or go be a server at a restaurant from 5:00 p.m. to midnight. Work for pay during those hours, and offer your time for free to the music label from nine to five. This is just my off-the-cuff advice; it's what I would do if I really wanted something and couldn't find a way in. Find a way to make some money, and go show the music labels what you've got."

He was definitely discouraged, but this was the best advice I had for him: to somehow make it work without giving up on his dream.

Fast forward fifteen years to the 2022 Super Bowl LVI at SoFi Stadium in Los Angeles. I was working as a bodyguard in a suite with two NFL team owners, some celebrities, and some big-name artists. The suites have floor-to-ceiling glass walls, so you can see into the other suites— what other people are eating and drinking, and who's there. Right before halftime, the security guy on the outside knocked on the door and told me there was someone outside who wanted to see me.

I stepped out in the hallway, and I remember thinking, "This guy looks familiar …" He reached out his hand, said his name, and introduced me to his beautiful wife. And then it hit me: this was the kid, fifteen years older, that I gave advice to at the GRAMMYs all those years ago.

He said he tried to track me down on and off for a couple of years after we first met. He told me, "Really, I have to thank you, man, for the advice you gave me to offer my services for free, to work as an intern, to do whatever I needed to get in the door."

It was easier said than done, but he made it happen. He called a music label multiple times and left messages. He kept calling until the receptionist finally picked up. She told him they didn't have any positions like the one he was looking for. He told her he would work for free, and she didn't believe him, but he kept saying, "Just let me work for free." Finally, to get rid of him, she told him to go see the HR director at their office in Santa Monica. So, he did. HR was also perplexed. No one could understand why he would work for free. He was persistent, and they finally agreed to let him work for free, doing odd tasks in the mailroom and filling in at the receptionist desk.

He learned as much as he could doing these odd jobs. He pitched his technical idea to a few people at the label, but they wrote him off as the nineteen-year-old kid who was working for free—what does he know? He was working late one Friday night when the vice president of business development was leaving the office and saw him at the front desk. He asked him what he was doing there so late, and he replied that he was studying everything he could about music and music labels. They chatted for about twenty minutes, and the VP was impressed—he could use someone like that in his department. So, the following Monday, he was on salary, working for that VP.

After about six months in that role, he left the label, having gotten as much as he could out of the job. They thought he was a little pie-in-the-sky dreamer and didn't take his ideas seriously. Eventually, he met someone from another label, pitched his idea, and struck gold. He started his own technical production company for the music industry. And at Super Bowl LVI, he was in the suite next to us because he had purchased it for the season. He was a multi-millionaire. And he said it was all because of the advice that I gave him.

He was kind of misty-eyed and crying. His wife was crying, and I thought, *Shit, I'm the bodyguard; I can't be crying.* He said, "If I hadn't taken that chance and offered my services for free, I would've been on a bus back to Minnesota. It was hard, but I worked for free for almost a year. And I worked at night, stocking shelves at Kroger until 2:00 a.m. because it was the only gig I could get." He thanked me profusely for being willing to talk to him.

What if I had dismissed him? Maybe he would've still fulfilled his dream, or maybe he would've ended up back at home with a completely different life. Maybe he would've given up because no one would give him the time of day. You never know how much even a short conversation can boost someone's confidence. Standing in that hallway, watching this successful entrepreneur thank me through tears, I realized I was witnessing the power of human connection. From a desperate kid looking to catch a break to a multi-millionaire in fifteen years—that transformation happened because someone chose to listen rather than walk away.

This is what relationship capital is all about. Relationship capital is very much related to servant leadership. It goes back to what I said about making more deposits than withdrawals in this figurative bank of relationships. There are times when relationship capital is better than cash money. The opportunities that a strong relationship can bring are endless. Little things don't just mean a lot; little things mean everything.

When I first started my bodyguard business, I was still a police officer. I wanted to make some extra money, and a retired sergeant that I knew named Jon owned a security company. Jon took a liking to me and wanted me to work for him on weekends and my days off. So, I started working for him part-time. This type of work was similar to the protection I provided in the Marine Corps. After working with Jon for some time, he was ready to retire, and I was ready to start a security business of my own. He helped me get it off the ground. He was very gracious in teaching me all the skills I needed to run a business myself.

My security business became a multi-million dollar business for me. And it all started because of a relationship that I built with someone. He trusted me and got to know me. Then he believed in me enough to give me an opportunity. That's relationship capital: taking the time to really get to know someone and understand how they work. Because he mentored me and built our relationship, I was able to start my own bodyguard business.

I like to think of the parts of the relationship capital cycle as follows: like, trust, transform, and scale. First, you get to know someone enough for them to like you. Then, they start to trust you. And once they trust you, that transforms your relationship, and you can then scale your business. A lot of people try to scale their businesses without implementing any of the other parts of the equation. That's a mistake. If someone doesn't like you, how are they ever going to trust you? Maybe you launch a product online and get a few sales, but you'll never get to the part where you're transforming lives if you don't first get people to like you and trust you.

With relationship capital, there are a lot of moving parts. You're building relationships with your customers but also with your employees. One important piece of advice I want to give you is to never dismiss somebody. Unfortunately, it's something we all do, and we have to pay attention. Can you think of a time when you were going about your day, and you brushed someone off? Maybe someone wants to talk to you for a minute, and you find a reason to cut them short, or maybe you don't engage at all. It's likely unintentional and without malice, but it happens.

I see it in business all the time. I see it with leadership. I encounter CEOs where an employee wants to talk to them for a minute, and they say, "Hey, let me catch you next week; I'm on my way to a meeting." This is why it's important to seek out opportunities to connect with your employees (and acquaintances and friends) so that you can have dedicated time to foster that connection.

To this day, I try to stop for anyone who wants a minute of my time, as long as it's reasonable. I'll either spare a few minutes for conversation, or I'll set up an appointment so we have more time to talk later. Sometimes people will approach you with crazy ideas or something you can't help them with. There are ways you can respond without hurting their feelings. I try my best to respectfully point people in another direction if I can't help them. The most important thing is to never dismiss someone because you never know how you might be helpful to someone or how that relationship might evolve.

We come in contact with dozens of people on a daily basis. At the gym, at work, at a social event, when traveling. Maybe you're in a position to help someone, but you don't know it until you talk to them. When someone tells you what they do for a living, it may not even be in the realm of your work, but there could be a potential partnership that you're not seeing. So many wonderful things—whether it's as simple as a friendship or as complex as a business venture—can come out of having a genuine conversation with someone.

To this day, I try to talk to as many people as I can. I'll ask the bagger at the grocery store what they want to be when they grow up. My friends make fun of me when we go out to restaurants because I'll ask the waiter or waitress if they have a dream they want to fulfill. And most of them will say yes, they're an actor or an actress, or they have this big idea. Sometimes they say they can't catch a break, and I offer them the same advice that I offered to that kid at the GRAMMYs. The least we can do is encourage people and offer them a bit of advice to help them accomplish their dreams. That's all part of being a great leader and a good human being.

There are all kinds of ways to help others and give back to your community. You can donate your money or your time and energy. You can give resources or recommendations. I volunteer with and donate to a couple of nonprofits, and I don't do it for accolades. I do it because I want to help. I have the time and the financial means. But people, even my wealthy friends, will often say that they'd love to help, but they "don't have the time."

Helping other people in some capacity just makes you feel good. And it's how you build connections. It all comes back to bringing value without expecting anything in return. While that's a principle of servant leadership, it also applies to relationship capital. Small acts of kindness cause a ripple effect in surprising and unexpected ways. You may find that meaningful connections and opportunities come from a simple gesture.

The guy who mentored me in the security business, Jon, was from England, and, right before the holidays every year, he would go to Costco and buy jars of English toffee by the hundreds. Then he would deliver them, in person, to all of his clients. He would leave them at the front desk with a note from him wishing them happy holidays. He drove all over town, dropping off jars of toffee to show his appreciation for their business. They liked him, he gained their trust, and he trans-formed their lives by not only being excellent at his job but also by showing his gratitude for them. And they, in turn, recommended him to everyone they knew, helping to scale his business. He multiplied his clients through this small act of kindness.

I started this same tradition with my own clients. I put my company's label on the jars, which I learned from Jon, and it was quite successful for my business and relationships as well. It doesn't matter what busi-ness you're in; make a meaningful gesture and leave people with something to remember you by. Show your appreciation. If you truly help someone with no expectations and build that relationship capital, it will come back to you tenfold.

Ask yourself this: have you been taking time to help others grow on their journey? Only you can answer truthfully. I think we could all answer honestly that we don't do enough. There are days I may ignore somebody if I'm preoccupied or stressed, but the GRAMMYs story lives in the back of my mind, reminding me of how good it feels to connect with others. Think about how offering someone a little help or a little advice could change the whole trajectory of their life.

If you're already contributing to the growth of your community, what is one way you can amplify your efforts and impact?

There's one thing I try to do every day: text three people, call three people, and email three people. Not for solicitations, just to check in and see how they're doing. To let them know I'm thinking about them. And when I say "call three people," I mean an actual bona fide phone call, not a voice message or a text. You can try this, too. If your parents are still alive, start there. Reconnect with an old friend from college, or your neighbor you haven't talked to in a while, or your old boss at the last company where you worked. Cultivate your relationships. Ask how they're doing or what's new in their life. Show interest because you care.

There's a difference between bringing value to a relationship with no expectation in return and a transactional relationship. Plenty of people make a living from transactional relationships, and that's fine, but it's important to know the difference. A lot of people I meet have a hard time understanding this. They'll say, "But I'm bringing them value; I'm providing a service." They're paying money for a service—that's the definition of a transaction. Truly bringing value to someone is helping them out or giving them advice without any expectations. You don't need to sign an NDA or other legal document to give someone advice.

Too many people I know rationalize in their minds that their work is more than transactional, yet they are not putting in the effort to build relationship capital. It's important to understand the difference between helping people without expecting anything in return and helping people who are paying you for a service or product. I promise you, though, that prioritizing the advice in this chapter will take your personal relationships and your business a lot farther than a mere transaction.

Transactional relationships have clear expectations: money for service, value for value. The GRAMMYs kid wasn't paying me for career advice, but that authentic moment of help generated far more value than any single transaction ever could. Every person you encounter this week, every seemingly ordinary interaction, could be your next meaningful connection. One genuine conversation could spark the next chapter of their story, or yours. Be open to the possibilities and opportunities standing right in front of you.

BUSINESS BITES

- **Everyone in your network is worth talking to.** Prioritize building authentic relationships with customers, employees, and partners. That delivery driver, receptionist, or junior employee might have connections you can't see. Make it a point to strike up a conversation with someone you might not normally talk to. You never know what kind of relationship might come from it.
- **Master the like-trust-transform-scale cycle.** You can't expect someone to trust you if they don't like you, and you definitely can't transform lives and scale your business without that foundation. If you try to scale without first establishing likability and trust, you're going to hurt your growth potential. Write down three ways that you implement this cycle in your business, side hustle, or even your 9-5.
- **Make relationship maintenance a daily habit.** The 3-3-3 approach (text three people, call three people, email three people every day) is a great way to consistently nurture your professional and personal networks. Don't only reach out to others when you need something. Building genuine rapport

with someone without expecting a business outcome goes a long way.

- **Know the difference between transactions and relationship capital.** If someone's paying you, that's a transaction. Real relationship capital happens when you help people with zero expectations—like giving advice to an inspiring entrepreneur or offering them a free product. People remember how you made them feel, not what you sold them.

CHAPTER 6
TRANSFORMING INTERACTIONS INTO OPPORTUNITIES

The way to compound on relationship capital is to interact with people every day and take the opportunity to offer them a small act of kindness. Whether you own a real estate company, a software company, or a café, people are coming in and out of your business, from clients to customers to potential employees to delivery drivers. You can offer a free bottle of water, a discounted product, or a helpful gadget with the name of your company on it. You can show gratitude to those who help you. And, in turn, that relationship can compound into opportunities.

Let me share a story that illustrates this principle in practice and just how far it can reach. One day, at Quest Nutrition headquarters, I walked by the front receptionist desk because I was looking for a package that hadn't yet arrived. Simultaneously, the FedEx driver walked in and dropped off a couple of things, not my delivery, though. He asked to use the restroom, and I directed him down the hallway. I asked the receptionist, "Do we provide water or anything for the people who deliver our mail and packages?" She told me no, that we only have a refrigerator to offer water to people who come in for job interviews or appointments. I suggested that we offer a beverage to *everyone* who walks through the door. I wanted to make it a company policy.

Then I took the idea one step further. I grabbed a couple of boxes of the protein bars and put them in the corner of the desk. I instructed the receptionist to give everyone who walked through the door some protein bars. By then, the FedEx driver was walking by again on his way out of the office, and I handed him a bottle of water and a couple of boxes of protein bars. He literally did not know what our company did. He said he saw the boxes of products and signage and always wondered. I thought, *Shame on us for not doing this sooner.* So, I told him a bit about the product, and he left with the two boxes.

The receptionist was completely on board. She said, "Bruce, you're so right; we need to do this for everyone. We need to show gratitude to everyone who comes through our front door."

About a month had gone by, and I was pulling into the office parking lot when I saw the same delivery driver walking out of the building. He stopped me and told me a crazy, amazing story. He told me he brought home the protein bars I gave him, and he and his wife tried them. She had seen them online but never bought any. His wife was a nurse practitioner and nutritionist at a hospital. She created diet plans for patients, and she loved the bars. She took some of them to work and shared them with the nurses and doctors on her floor. She wanted to know how to get the bars stocked in the hospital gift shop. So she just asked the gift shop manager if he would sell them, and he agreed.

Then one day, a surgeon who tried the bars told her they were amazing. He was an investor and owned a CrossFit gym across town, where he thought the bars would sell well. So she pointed him to the website, and he started carrying the bars at his gym. The FedEx driver and his nurse practitioner wife had three daughters who played soccer. When it was their turn to provide snacks, she bought some boxes of Quest Nutrition protein bars and brought them to soccer practice. All the girls and their parents tried the bars. One of the dads owned a handful of health clinics, and he decided to stock them at the front desks at all his clinics.

The protein bars made it into the hands of all those different people and businesses, all because we gave a couple of boxes to the FedEx driver, and he and his wife liked them enough to share them. This is a trickle-down effect in action. I created a document, almost like an organizational chart or a relationship tree, to show all the exposure to the product from that one initial interaction. We couldn't track the relationship capital that came from that particular interaction, but I suspect it resulted in thousands of dollars in sales.

The CrossFit gym owner. The health clinic owner. The hospital gift shop. The soccer families. The patients in the hospital. The list goes on and on. There's no telling how many more people learned about the product and liked it. And all because I decided to show an act of kindness to a guy who was working really hard. I never once thought of it as a marketing tactic. But it did end up being great marketing for the business. Because it was a like, trust, transform, scale situation. I was friendly with and thankful to the FedEx driver, and I earned his trust, and then he and his wife wanted to share the product, and that action transformed people's lives and scaled the exposure of Quest Nutrition protein bars.

The FedEx driver came inside and told the story to the receptionist as well. She couldn't believe it, and it made her more excited to share the product. She would randomly text me, telling me who had come into the office and that she had given products to them.

This experience was an example of organic customer service at its finest. It reinforced for me that customer service is a philosophy that should be at the forefront of all of your business decisions. I recently heard Jeff Bezos say that if you become obsessed with customer service, you'll never have to worry about your competition. I have to second that sentiment; being obsessed with your customers is paramount to your business. Don't worry about your competition. Focus instead on your customers and show them gratitude and appreciation. The minute you stop thinking about your customers and worrying about your competition is when things start to fall apart in your business.

We've all eaten at a restaurant that was disappointing, right? Then maybe you're at soccer camp with your kids or getting coffee with a friend, and someone says, "What did you do this weekend?" And your response is that you went to a terrible restaurant that you wouldn't recommend to anyone. You may end up telling ten friends about this bad experience. When you have a good experience somewhere, you may also tell a few close friends, or you may tell no one. The experiences you have define you. And we're just as likely, if not more so, to share a bad experience as we are to share a good one.

In my experience, there are very few brands that truly put their customers first. Some that are top of mind for me include American Express, Four Seasons Hotels, 1st Phorm Nutrition, Quest Nutrition, and Reebok. When I purchase items and receive a personalized note, that's good customer service right there. It doesn't happen often anymore. Without your customers, you have nothing. So, investing in good customer service is one of the best things you can do. Handwritten notes, phone calls, texts, emails—those personal touches let your customer know how much you appreciate them.

Early in my time at Quest Nutrition, I had the good fortune to meet Tony Hsieh, the founder of Zappos and author of *Delivering Happiness*. The company sent some product to someone on his team, and his assistant reached out to invite me to spend time with him. It was amazing. I came back to Los Angeles with marching orders—not from him, but from myself, based on advice that he gave me. He told me that people want to do business with people they like. You could have a product that's just okay, but if they like you, they'll overlook any glitches that may come up if they like doing business with you, and you respond promptly and give them good customer service. That says a lot about relationships and delivering happiness. Keep that in mind.

Now, I'm not telling you to sell a subpar product. What I'm saying is that relationships are the most important thing, period. If you have a great customer service experience, you may overlook an issue. But if you have a bad customer service experience, how many people are you going to tell?

People ask me all the time how companies, such as Quest Nutrition, go from being worth millions to billions. The key is acquiring customers for life. Lifetime customers aren't easy to come by, right?

Sometimes someone makes a one-time purchase and likes it, but they might go back to their old brand or keep trying new brands, switching up their purchases. This behavior does not make someone a lifetime customer.

So, what *does* make someone a lifetime customer? Brand consistency. And what builds a consistent, successful brand? Your customers. It doesn't happen overnight; it can take years for this to happen. It requires one customer to tell the next, and on and on, until it catches, and your customers multiply.

The secret to creating this kind of loyalty stems from the "Thousand True Fans" theory, which was coined in a 2008 essay by Kevin Kelly. The idea is that your true fans will be there for the long haul. These are your customers for life. Now, how do you keep them around? When people like you, they listen. When they trust you, they buy. But when you transform their life, they'll go to the highest mountaintops and shout your name.

These fans will be loyal and diehard, and then they're going to tell ten friends, and those ten friends will tell ten friends, and so on. That's how you go from 1,000 screaming fans to 10,000 to 100,000. And that's what you need to build a million- or billion-dollar brand.

At Quest, we had a very simple formula to build a loyal following that became lifetime customers. There's a reason this exact model works flawlessly for both consumable brands as well as services and experiences. It's about prioritizing brand consistency over brand creativity. We got the product into people's hands in any way that we could. We would hand out samples at events and conferences. Anyone who asked, we would mail them two complimentary bars. This is how we got feedback on what people want in a protein bar. Our customers were buying a product from us that is part of their everyday lives. Being consistent in our approach not only benefited our company but also benefited our clients.

Sure, there were attempts at creativity along the way, but the truth is that none of them panned out. There were some people in the company who thought creativity was more important than consistency, which resulted in some pretty epic, costly failures. Let's walk through a few of them:

Music video: Someone had the idea to launch a music video to announce a new protein bar flavor: blueberry muffin. A three-day musical production ensued, with influencers, dancers, singers, and choreographers. We filmed at studios and venues around the greater Los Angeles area. A lot, and I mean a lot, of money—somewhere around $700,000, if memory serves me correctly—and time went into this endeavor, but our sales numbers remained the same. This music video did not bring in new customers.

Food truck: We also outfitted a food truck to take to events to sell our protein shakes. We didn't really utilize the food truck to its fullest potential, and that initial excitement quickly fizzled out. We didn't develop the idea as well as we could have.

In-house TV show: We were already providing healthy food for the body, and someone in the upper ranks suggested we provide healthy information for the mind. This TV show had a complete production team, including directors, producers, production assistants, and sound engineers. We had weekly guests—among them influencers, thought leaders, scientists, and authors. We had to set up a production studio/soundstage in the back of our humble headquarters to accommodate this endeavor. Everyone in the company had to be available for the tapings of the snow, and those in charge would be infuriated if we weren't there. If I had to make an educated guess, I would say we spent at least $10,000 per episode, and that's not including employee time spent watching the tapings instead of getting product into people's hands and talking to them about the brand.

Virtual reality booth: One year, at the Olympia Fitness & Performance Weekend in Las Vegas, we set up a virtual reality booth. As people entered the booth, they put on virtual reality glasses and went through a series of simulations. This slowed down the process of giving samples to people and getting their feedback. I think we calculated that we handed out maybe a third of the samples we normally would have. The goal is to get as many samples as possible into people's hands over the two-day event. A booth at an expo like Olympia is a tremendous investment, and it was wasted that year.

The moral here is that, in these instances, people were trying to make Quest Nutrition into something other than a protein bar company. We weren't musicians or producers or in the food services business. We had a really good product, and at the end of the day, keeping our marketing and branding focus consistent is what kept customers around. There's really no downside to consistent branding, other than it may feel boring and mundane day in and day out. People think they need to change things up and get creative, when in reality, focusing on delivering a stellar product or service should be your number one priority.

At the height of our success, we created what we called the Knowledge and Training Department, responsible for new-hire orientation for full-time employees as well as ambassadors and athletes. I believe this department was the most heavily staffed, with at least ten employees.

We learned that this department was misrepresenting the company's origin story to new employees and ambassadors. Their teaching methodology was also shocking—they had new employees making figures out of playdough instead of learning about the importance of nutrition and macros. Changes were made, and certain people separated from Quest Nutrition, and this department was disbanded forever. We, again, went back to what we knew was best: consistency and accuracy. We hired athletes, nutritionists, and trainers to instill the necessary knowledge needed for the employees, ambassadors, and athletes.

Overstaffing wasn't limited to this department only; it was a company-wide problem for a while. We had a running joke that personal assistants were hiring their own personal assistants—it wasn't quite that bad, but it was close. At one point, I went to the founders and told them I thought we were hiring too many people without solid job responsibilities. It was getting out of control. This overstaffing was a really glaring problem. People milling around with nothing to do weren't helping us get the product into customers' hands.

I remember someone on the team hired an assistant and, on her first day, said to her, "My lunch is in that refrigerator. At noon, and I mean exactly noon on the dot, take out the two containers and put the chicken and broccoli on a plate, warm them up for three minutes, and place the meal on my desk. Are we clear?"

This was perhaps one of the most humiliating things I've ever witnessed happen to a human being. Needless to say, at the end of her first day, she gracefully and professionally resigned, telling the director of HR that she wasn't hired to warm up someone's lunch.

All this excessive hiring was a distraction. A distraction from where the company's focus needed to be: the product. Just like the music video and the TV show, overstaffing was another example of losing sight of what actually mattered: getting our product into customers' hands and listening to their feedback. Even with the best intentions of listening to customers, mistakes can happen. I want to highlight a mistake made at Quest Nutrition that temporarily hurt the brand and took us a long time to recover from.

Ron and the team discovered, after learning about a report, that our fiber source was not accurate and our labels were misleading in reporting correct calories and carbohydrates. It was important that our product maintain integrity, so the team immediately made the decision to switch to a different fiber source with accurate nutrition information. This, in the long run, was better for the brand and the product.

Unfortunately, the taste and texture were not as appealing to our customers. They noticed the change immediately, and the fallout came pretty swiftly and steadily. I was traveling every weekend promoting the product. At trade shows and in-store visits, I kept hearing firsthand from customers how disappointed they were in the change to the bars. People felt like we had cheapened the product.

Back in the office, the numbers hadn't yet reflected the disapproval of our customers. Sales were still brisk and strong. I was trying to get ahead of falling sales, but in the end, I wasn't successful. Our sales went from about $440 million a year to almost $300 million a year. It took a very long time to recover, and, even then, we never got back to our record $440 million a year in sales before the company sold. The moral of the story here is to listen to your customers. They're the ones spending the money on your product and telling others about it and sharing it with friends. How can they be your screaming fans if you don't listen to what they have to say?

I think it's just as important to point out failures as it is to point out successes. You will undoubtedly encounter challenging times as an entrepreneur or business owner. Stay focused on the objective at hand: building your brand in the most efficient, cost-effective, and meaningful way possible. That being said, I do want to acknowledge that we had a lot of success at Quest. We received award after award, including Protein Bar of the Year from both GNC and The Vitamin Shoppe. In 2014, we were named by Inc. 5000 as the second fastest-growing company in the United States, with 57,000 percent growth. An interesting sidenote: The company that was named number one that year ended up going out of business the next year. Many publications and articles name ours as the favorite protein bar of choice. I would say the accolades and rewards and true acknowledgment from the industry as a whole far outweigh any of the shortcomings we had.

QUEST NUTRITION RANKED NO. 2 ON THE 2014 INC. 5000 LIST

Ranking:
Quest Nutrition was the second-fastest-growing company on the 2014 Inc. 5000 list.

Growth:
Within its first three years, the company experienced a growth rate of 57,000%.

Revenue:
It achieved revenues of $82.6 million by 2014.

Quest Nutrition was acquired by Simply Good Foods Co. for $1 billion in 2019.

Source: The Inc. 5000

Brand consistency relies on keeping your product or service the best that it can be. We did this at Quest Nutrition with our brand ambassador and athlete program. We recruited people who saw firsthand the movement we were creating because they were customers. They wanted to be even more involved in the journey—the quest, if you will. It is a true blessing to have people who believe in your mission and your values become megaphones for your movement.

We prioritized consistent communication with our ambassadors and athletes. That consistency resonated across the country, with the same messaging, core values, and even sampling practices at every event and every expo we attended. I didn't realize how unique this phenomenon was until I saw other brands at the same events, doing demos. I personally witnessed the lack of excitement in the faces of other brand ambassadors. We were blessed to have such a unique, loyal fan base that represented us so proudly.

We never took advantage of that, and we definitely went out of our way to acknowledge the hard work and efforts of those ambassadors and athletes who represented us on the front lines. Every day, they were our voices, our megaphones, our mouthpieces. They weren't polished spokespeople; they were fans, athletes, creators, and everyday people who loved the product and lived the lifestyle. Their stories carried more weight than any commercial ever could because they were real.

I will drive home that if a brand wants to reach a high level of success, it's important to recruit and attract like-minded people who believe not only in your mission but also in the products you produce. They have to stand by you 100 percent. Quest Nutrition grew because people felt connected to the brand. They saw themselves in the mission. They weren't just customers; they were part of a family that shared the same goals: to get better, to live better, and to inspire others to do the same.

If you are fortunate enough to attract the kind of talent we did at Quest, embrace it. You will find that brand ambassadors will come and go, and that's okay. At Quest, we had ones that stayed, and we looked for opportunities for them to grow within the company— anywhere from R&D to marketing to creative. We invested in them.

When people are genuinely proud to wear your logo, share your story, and stand for your purpose, that's when a brand truly takes off. That excitement becomes magnetic, and it keeps growing because it's authentic.

We used to say at Quest Nutrition that people would bleed Quest blue for us. We actually had several people get tattoos, including the event's director, who worked for me, who got the word "Quest" tattooed on her wrist. I'm proud to say that we have the same level of loyalty at Legendary Foods, and in some ways, it's even been easier to connect people with our mission.

At the end of the day, transforming interactions into opportunities isn't about a viral moment or an out-there marketing idea; it's about showing up for your customers with kindness, consistency, and a willingness to learn and grow. Every interaction is a seed. And your customers will help you build a brand and a following that may exceed even your biggest aspirations if you let them.

So whether you're building a new brand or expanding a legacy one, remember this: authenticity isn't a strategy; it's your story. It's your people, your culture, your purpose. When your team, your ambassadors, and your community believe in what you're building—like we did at Quest Nutrition and now Legendary Foods—your brand doesn't just grow; it becomes a movement.

BUSINESS BITES

- **Show gratitude to everyone you meet.** Whether it's a delivery driver, a vendor, or a walk-in customer, treat them with genuine kindness. Offer them something, whether it's a sample of your product or a kind word. You never know where that relationship will lead or how many doors it might open.
- **Stop worrying about your competition and start obsessing over your customers.** Pour your energy into making people feel appreciated. Go the extra mile to deliver a product or

service that meets their needs and desires. When customers feel valued, they'll stick with you—and tell others.

- **Prioritize consistency over creativity—even when it feels boring.** It's tempting to chase flashy marketing ideas, but if they don't get your product into more customers' hands, they're just expensive distractions. Before launching any new initiative, ask yourself: *Does this help us do what we do best, or are we trying to be something we're not?* Master consistency first, and stay focused on your mission to avoid unnecessary failures.

- **Stay lean and focused on what drives results.** It's easy to add staff and develop initiatives that *seem* productive but don't directly serve customers or support the brand. Before hiring a bunch of people or creating a new department, ask yourself, "Will this effort get our service or product more exposure or help us better listen to customer feedback?" If the answer is no, get back to the basics.

- **Your customers are your best advisors—listen to them.** They're the ones using your product and telling others about it. When they speak up with feedback, pay attention. Ignoring what they're telling you can cost you more than you realize and take years to recover from. Don't just make a sale; make an impact.

CHAPTER 7
BUILDING DISCIPLINE AND WORK ETHIC

As I've already mentioned, my father's influence instilled in me values that developed into a strong work ethic over time. I started working at age twelve. We had a pretty good life, so while I didn't *have* to work at such a young age, I *wanted* to. I liked having a little extra money in my pocket, but it wasn't the money I was chasing. I was chasing the experience and the knowledge I'd gain from the experience.

The desire to know more was fueled by my childlike curiosity. Just because we are no longer children doesn't mean there is nothing left to learn. Our innate human desire to explore has no limitations, including age. Curiosity leads to growth, and growth leads to success. If you strive to never lose your sense of wonder, you'll never stop growing. Curiosity can be a powerful tool toward building a solid work ethic.

My desire for knowledge is what led me to begin my first entrepreneurial journey. At twelve years old, I began my own newspaper route, where I got my first taste of what it means to be responsible and where I learned the value of saving and making money. As simple as delivering papers was, I remember every detail of it, clear as day. My customers expected their paper to be dropped off before 5:00

p.m., and some were more strict than others. Long before cell phones, some of those customers would call my house phone directly to ask my mother where I was if I didn't drop it off by 5:00 p.m. on the dot. Inevitably, weather circumstances such as ice, rain, and snow would often cause delays, but I still got those papers delivered.

I had the amazing experience, at a young age, of learning what it meant to be relied on and responsible for other people's needs, not just my own. It taught me the value of focus and hard work and the importance of executing on promises made. I learned to prioritize my customers' needs and wants so they enjoyed a positive experience. No matter the task, I knew I had a duty, and my work ethic only grew from there.

After working my paper route for three years, I went on to work at a local market and butcher shop owned by two immigrant brothers, Albert and Arnold Gasparri. This job played another really pivotal role in my life. I worked as a stock boy making minimum wage. While my father taught me the essential foundation to a long-lasting work ethic, the Gasparri brothers continued to light that flame for me. They were kind, hard-working people, and they didn't have a lot of money. That motivated me to be as dedicated as possible to helping them build their business. They didn't only provide me with an opportunity to work, they provided me with new knowledge. After hours, they would teach me additional skills, like how to properly cut and trim meat and how to safely use a meat grinder. They gave me the opportunity to grow, to learn something beyond stocking shelves. The Gasparri brothers made an unforgettable impact on me in more ways than one, especially Arnold. As a veteran, his advice played an instrumental role in my decision to eventually enlist in the Marine Corps. I remembered the lessons about work ethic that he shared with me as a kid from his days as a Marine.

My dad's work ethic also impacted not only my professional life, but also my personal life. To say he was a role model of a father is an understatement. By involving himself in every aspect of my life, I was shown the true meaning of what it means to be there for your children. I always had someone to look up to, no matter what I was doing.

When I joined a sport, he stepped up as the assistant coach. When I became a Boy Scout, he served as our Boy Scout troop leader. He loved the Boy Scouts, and being a leader became a calling for him for the rest of his life. He was honored and presented with awards from congressmen and senators for his participation in the organization.

I was proud of him for his integrity and interest in giving back to the community. I also know that it was important to him to stay connected with us during our childhood and into our teen years; he significantly valued and prioritized our time together. He was so glad to step up, and that's what made his efforts so admirable. He was my role model, and I watched and learned from his example.

There is even a section of a 15-mile hiking trail that runs through High Bridge that was named after my dad and my mom because of their involvement in the community. The Columbia Trail, once a booming railway route through our hometown, was converted into a hiking, biking, and running trail. My parents regularly received recognition for their community contributions throughout my childhood, making an honor such as this one particularly meaningful to me.

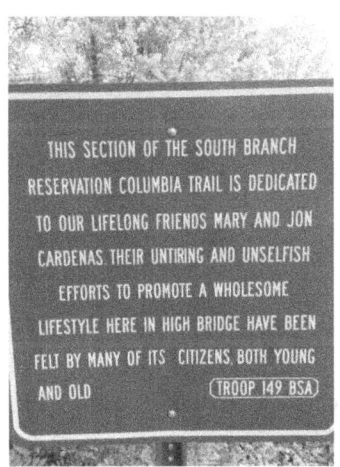

Plaque dedicating a section of the Columbia Trail to Bruce's parents, Mary and Jon Cardenas

Behind most ambitious children who feel confident exploring their curiosity is often a strong support system. As Boy Scouts, to earn our badges, we had to work on a meaningful project. I had an idea and presented it to my father. The city did not have a recycling program, so we decided to start one. I thought that creating a marketing plan would help because there was no outreach to the community at the time. I asked my father if we could present my plan to the city. He never failed to welcome my curiosity with positivity. The city was very happy for me to volunteer my time to promote the recycling program. This became my Boy Scout project, and my father helped me with it every Saturday.

We marketed the program with fliers I created by going door-to-door to every home and business in High Bridge. We knocked, handed each person a flyer, and gave our rehearsed marketing pitch: "Hello! Did you know you can drop off your glass and paper at the recycling center every Saturday morning? No need to sort it; I'll be there to do that for you, along with the other Boy Scouts in my troop. Less work for you and more space in your bins! Plus, recycling is a great cause for the environment."

It was a win-win situation for everyone. It saved people time, which they loved. It helped me build my work ethic and understanding of responsibility. And it benefited my Boy Scout troop. At the time, the city was paid money for recycling materials. So, part of the deal was that they gave a percentage to my troop for our work, which in turn meant we could put our share of the profits toward our fifty-mile hikes, canoe trips, and other activities that needed funding.

By the first Saturday, people were pouring in with loads of material to be recycled. Our troop arrived bright and early to separate items, put them into bins, and prepare for the scheduled pickup the following Monday. This recycling program eventually developed into a business that continued for many years after I moved away. Not too shabby for my first taste of dealing with the government, if you will. Even though I wasn't personally compensated for our work, the outcome was worth it. I created a business opportunity, and with my dad and fellow Boy Scouts, we brought money back into our organization. I call that a success.

I couldn't have been more than fifteen years old when I created and orchestrated that marketing plan. Of course, at the beginning, my father did his fair share behind the scenes to ensure everything ran smoothly. But once we were up and running, he let me take the reins to facilitate all the details. He helped me prepare for my presentation at the city council meeting, but I presented my business idea all by myself. I was so proud to walk out of that meeting with their approval to pursue it.

If you have kids or you mentor young people, I recommend that you encourage them to take advantage of opportunities to volunteer or work at a young age. The worst that could happen is that they're told "No," but that's not a bad thing. Naturally, most of us have been conditioned to dislike, or even fear, that word of rejection ever since we were toddlers. The truth is, every "no" gets you one step closer to success.

No matter what age you are, the more you put yourself in situations that leave you vulnerable to rejection, the less afraid of rejection you will be. The goal is to no longer fear rejection, because without fear holding you back, what's stopping you from shooting your shot? Opportunities are everywhere, and opportunists don't wait for their "once in a lifetime shot" to magically show up on a silver platter. Instead, they risk the possibility of rejection and chase the shot down themselves.

Discipline goes a long way. Go after what you want, no matter what. It's admittedly difficult to be fully committed and to execute your vision and plan, no matter the pain points along the way. I think that's why a lot of people quit when things get tough. They weren't trained or properly conditioned to see things through to the end. The difficulties become overwhelming, and they give up. Discipline is how you execute and stay the course. Passion comes and goes, and sometimes the path is not clear. But discipline is a lifelong skill, a muscle that you have to exercise regularly to keep your vision and your dreams alive.

Discipline is hard, but it's lasting if we stick with it. For example, I wake up every morning at the same time; it's a habit I have built. I meet my training partner at 7 a.m., rain or shine, no matter what. Even if I don't feel good, or I'm tired, or I'm sore, I go. I've created a discipline around working out because it's important to me. I could certainly come up with a lot of excuses for not going. Am I passionate about my 7 a.m. workout routine? Not always. Some days, I'm pumped up about setting a new bench pressing record, and other days, I just flat out don't want to go. But it's an important part of my life for my health, mental stress, and physical ability. I have disciplined myself to make this a priority in my life.

The same applies to business. I've been very fortunate with my business opportunities, as I've found passion and purpose in much of the work I do. This may be the case for you as well, or it might not. You have to show up to your job every single day. Maybe you love it, or maybe you're in a job right now that you're not passionate about while you are building a side hustle that you love. If you don't have passion for what you're doing, or you just have some off days—which happens to the best of us—you need the discipline to accomplish your work.

Whether you're an employee, an independent contractor, a department leader, or a CEO, discipline will carry you through the days when the passion just isn't there. I promise you, even the most successful people wake up on days when passion is not the first thing on their mind. The first thing on their mind may be stress, despair, or discouragement, but they wake up disciplined, knowing they have to push through this pain to see through to the other side. As the saying goes, "The only way out is through."

Executing on a goal requires focus and determination. When you stick to the plan, the responsibilities, and the deadlines, that's discipline in action. Ask yourself this: Are you disciplined when no one is looking? It may sound silly, but discipline can be applied to something as simple as making your bed every morning. You. Alone in your room. No one is watching or expecting anything of you. Do you make your bed? If you *do* wake up and make your bed, you're likely to start the day feeling good. You already accomplished a simple task before getting your day started. If you don't make your bed, nothing bad is going to happen, but it may set your day up to not feel as good. Or it may be difficult for you to build more meaningful habits if you don't first discipline yourself to do the little things.

Attacking everything in your life—from making your bed to starting a business—with discipline and commitment to the best of your abilities is nothing but a rewarding feeling of satisfaction, to be honest.

The discipline I've developed over the years taught me something crucial about how successful businesses actually operate. All the discipline in the world won't matter if you're not applying it in the right role. Through my professional experiences, I've learned that the most successful companies aren't built by people trying to do everything themselves. Instead, they're built by partnerships where each person focuses their disciplined effort on what they do best. This brings me to one of the most important distinctions I've discovered in business.

In business, there are visionaries and integrators. Dreamers and doers.

A visionary (dreamer) is someone who generates and communicates a compelling vision for the future, often with innovative ideas and long-term goals. They excel at visualizing the big picture and the final product or goal. They are typically creative thinkers who see possibilities beyond the current state.

An integrator (doer), on the other hand, is someone who excels at bringing ideas and plans to fruition by organizing, resourcing, coordinating efforts, and ensuring alignment with the overall vision. Integrators are skilled at execution and operating under the vision set forth by the visionary. They have strong attention to detail, enjoy processes and procedures, and perfecting them over time, and are not burdened by the work it takes to achieve success.

In essence, the visionary sets the direction and inspires others, while the integrator turns that vision into reality through practice, implementation, and coordination.

Steve Jobs was a perfect example of a visionary. He was a truly horrible integrator, though; he couldn't keep his team together. If it weren't for Steve Wozniak, Jobs would not have had a successful company. Jobs was the visionary, and Wozniak was the integrator.

The leadership team at Quest Nutrition is a great example as well. Ron had an amazing vision for these protein bars that were going to change the world. But he also needed Mike Osborn, who was the operations guy behind the scenes, integrating all the moving pieces—the production, the equipment, and the financing—together to turn the vision into reality.

In an ideal world, your business has a solid partnership with a visionary and an integrator. The problem that a lot of business owners face is that they try to wear both hats. On rare occasions, it can work, but for the most part, one person does not fit both roles. You can dream and talk, but until you take action, nothing will happen.

Visionaries have to be risk takers because there's no promise of anything. Every great business started with a vision and a dream. Finding the right team to help you execute is how you succeed at making a dream a reality. Think about it. Shannan was making these protein bars by hand in their kitchen. And Ron had the business acumen to realize they could commercialize them. Without Ron's vision to take it to the next level, the bars would've probably sold fine. Shannan may still be making them in her kitchen, selling them to her friends. If it wasn't for Ron's vision to turn it into a commercial business opportunity, there may never have been a Quest Nutrition as the world knows it today.

The most important question to ask yourself is, are you a visionary or an integrator? It's as simple as answering that one question. You can't pretend to be both. Now that you understand the difference between the two types of people, it should be easy to tell which you are.

Now, consider for a minute how you can implement your ideas. What can you do to set the wheels in motion? Find a friend or mentor who believes in your dreams, and work to make them a reality. Don't let your dream die a slow death because you didn't have the discipline and the vision to at least take the next step. If you're a visionary, find an integrator to help you get your idea off the ground. And if you're an integrator, find a visionary with an idea you're passionate about. Together, these two leaders can build something exciting.

It may all start with a dream, but you still need the discipline to start executing. I know there's someone out there with the next best idea— in real estate or nutrition or fitness or arts and culture or travel—just waiting to get started. They're just not executing on it. And to all those who work a nine-to-five and say that they don't have the time, I'll remind you that nine to five is a small window of time. What are you doing at 5 p.m. when you log out of work? Instead of going to get that glass of wine, start building your website. You just have to get over the hump and start. Find thirty minutes or an hour wherever you can to work towards your dream.

It can be as simple as getting together with a couple of your friends who share similar ideals and starting an LLC. Come up with an idea, decide who the visionaries and the integrators are, and start a company. It really is that simple. The worst-case scenario is that you fail, which just means you learned something for the next endeavor. The best-case scenario is that you become a millionaire or that you find your purpose in life.

BUSINESS BITES

- **Passion is nothing without discipline.** Passion is an important factor in doing something you care about, but it comes and goes. Discipline is what gets you to show up when you don't feel like it. Start by implementing three simple habits each day that you can build on. How you do one thing is how you do everything.
- **Embrace rejection as your teacher.** Every "no" gets you one step closer to success. The more you put yourself in situations where you might get rejected, the less you'll fear it. Stop waiting for opportunities to show up on a silver platter— chase them down yourself. If you put yourself out there and receive a "no," take a moment to celebrate what you learned. And then move on.
- **Know whether you're a visionary or an integrator.** You can't pretend to be both. Visionaries have ambitious dreams and can see the big picture. Integrators execute and turn those dreams into reality. Which one are you? Write down a list of your strengths/weaknesses and the kind of work that you gravitate towards. This will help you discover which type

of person you are, so you can focus on executing within your unique skill set.

- **Start executing, even if it's just 30 minutes a day.** Stop making excuses about not having time after your nine-to-five. A little effort goes a long way towards your goals. Schedule time on your calendar and make it non-negotiable, just as you would with a meeting for work. Set a reminder on your phone. Whatever you need to do to ensure you take action on finding those small pockets of time to work toward your dreams.

- **Take action before you're ready.** It's easy to be scared, and it's even easier to make excuses. Do the thing scared. Take the risk. The worst that happens is you learn from the experience, and that's never a bad thing. Pick one scary thing, write it down, put it somewhere prominent, and do it. You're now one step closer to your goals.

> 66
>
> **The most dangerous person in the world is the one who continues to show up every day even when the rewards are not guaranteed.**
>
> **Your potential is determined by the amount of uncertainty you're able to tolerate and how long you can tolerate it for.**
>
> *– Alex Hormozi*

CHAPTER 8
OWNING YOUR WORK TO OWN YOUR SUCCESS

T hings were going great at Quest Nutrition when we experienced a bit of a snafu. There was a formulation issue that caused the bars to harden after sitting on the shelves. The bars got recalled. Thousands of stores stocked our bars, and truckloads of product were returned to headquarters during this time.

Talk about a setback. We turned it into a learning opportunity. We worked long and hard to reformulate and test the bars and come back strong. We took ownership of the situation. We had pride in the company and the protein bars, and so we put in the work to rectify the issue. Embracing setbacks as learning opportunities is the best way to approach them, because they will happen. If you have the right mindset and values, failure is just a stepping stone on the way to success.

I previously discussed the impact of the core values I learned in the Marines: honor, courage, and commitment. Those values have been a foundation for me to take pride and ownership in everything I've done. They've taught me to take pride in my work, to lead with purpose, and to hold myself to the highest standards, even when emotions or circumstances might pull me in another direction.

Being an entrepreneur is not easy, and you're going to have setbacks. That's why it's so important to have pride and ownership in your work. Having a set of standards by which you run your company means you will dive in and take charge if those standards become subpar. That might mean rolling up your sleeves as the CEO or founder and getting into the trenches to solve a problem. Leading by example is a way to take ownership and show pride in your work. It wasn't until I started running my own business that I realized the importance of this. If you want others—your business partners, your employees, or even your customers—to take pride in your company, you have to be the first to demonstrate what that looks like.

Pride and ownership are about selling. Even though a company is made up of a lot of different roles, at the end of the day, everyone's job is sales. You're all contributing to selling a service, a product, or an experience. From marketing to product to HR, everyone is selling. And when your employees want to sell, when they want to talk up your company, that means they have pride and ownership in what you're doing.

In my bodyguard business, I always made it a point to be on site and show my team how to conduct themselves. People will grasp their responsibilities better when you show them. If you want to be a good leader, you're going to get your hands dirty sometimes. You can't assume people will know what you want or how to perform a task to your standards unless you show them exactly what your expectations are. You will set yourself and your team up for success when you involve everyone in feeling like an authority on the trajectory of your business.

I like to think of success as a bicycle wheel—a structure where every spoke is essential to keeping it strong and moving forward. A single spoke, no matter how sturdy, can't support the wheel on its own. But when all the spokes work together in harmony, the wheel gains balance, strength, and the ability to propel forward. This metaphor captures the essence of success in business: every person, every department, and every action plays a critical role in the journey as a whole.

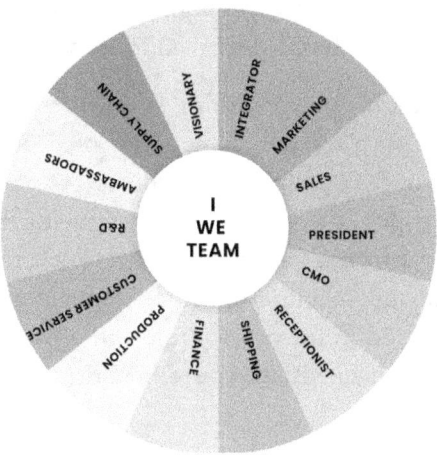

My experience at Quest Nutrition is a great example. Every single person at the company was vital to its success. From the receptionist who greeted everyone with warmth, to the shipping team ensuring timely deliveries, to the HR professionals fostering a strong company culture, to the sales reps forging new relationships, and the marketing team amplifying the company's voice—every role mattered. I was just one spoke in the wheel. My role was one of deep commitment, always focused on making the wheel turn. But it was never just about me—it was about *us*.

At Quest Nutrition, we embraced the power of "we." We understood that our collective strength turned the wheel of success, driving us toward our shared vision. Just like a perfectly crafted bicycle wheel, every spoke mattered, ensuring that our ride was smooth, stable, and unstoppable. Together, as a team, we built something extraordinary.

There are three types of people in every company. The **"minor players"** are the 9-to-5ers who do their job well without making waves. Every company has them, and every company needs them. The **"progress go-getters"** think outside the box and aren't afraid to shake things up. They're the ones who get you to the finish line—the more you have, the faster you grow. Then there are the **"impediment**

makers." They cause friction and argue just to be right. Identify and replace them quickly to stay on the road to success.

The best advice I can give on hiring is to hire slowly and fire fast. Never hire based on a resume alone. A lot of people embellish their resumes, plus you can't really learn about work ethic or cultural fit from a piece of paper. There's nothing wrong with the courting phase during the hiring process. Pay someone to work a thirty- or sixty-day trial period; if it's not working out, don't extend an offer. You want someone to be a good fit for your culture and organization. When you build your team with intention, you're investing in everyone's success, not just your own.

In life and in business, people often fall into the trap of saying "me, me, me," forgetting that genuine success is rarely achieved in isolation. Unfortunately, many people who start a business make the mistake of thinking it's a one-person show. They believe that their vision, their hustle, and their brilliance alone will carry them to the finish line. Without the support and contributions of a team, even the best ideas risk falling flat.

If you want to succeed, you must take ownership of all of your actions, good or bad. This concept is known as "extreme ownership" and is discussed in one of my favorite books, *Extreme Ownership: How U.S. Navy SEALs Lead and Win* by Jocko Willink and Leif Babin. Great leaders have to be the front line for holding themselves accountable. It can be difficult. But success doesn't care about your comfort. You must push forward with discipline, driven by your purpose, regardless of the challenges. That, my friends, is what separates success from mediocrity.

Do you know what happens in Japanese corporations if there's a lack of performance, output, or profit, or if there's low employee morale? The guy at the top goes. They don't fire mid-level managers or entry-level employees. They get rid of the person at the top of the company. As a leader, the pride and ownership that others have depend on the pride and ownership that you have to make the business successful. Take extreme ownership in everything that happens at your company. If there's an HR issue or a disgruntled employee or a financial discrepancy, it all comes back to you. This principle was put to the ultimate test when my thriving business hit a speed bump that I wasn't prepared for. Imagine if American companies operated like this.

My bodyguard business had been doing incredibly well financially, and we were experiencing tremendous growth. I knew how to bring in business and how to get the job done. The trouble was that I didn't understand the backend of the business. I received a call one day from Renee, my bookkeeper, about payroll. I thought it was weird because she usually never called me about that; she always sent out the checks with no issue. But this time, there was an issue. She said, "Bruce, payroll is due on Friday, and it's $75,000, like always. But there's only $25,000 in the bank. The money is not coming in quickly enough to keep making payroll." She then listed some of our clients who still owed me money, including studios and record labels.

The funny thing is, I was doing quite well financially. The year before, I bought my mother a brand new car with cash. That was one of the greatest joys in the world for me, by the way. I was finally able to do something meaningful for my mother after all the years she took care of me. Now here I was a year later, and I couldn't make payroll? I started calling the clients who owed me money to see if they could pay me earlier than usual to cover the deficit. But that's not how the real world works. They basically said to me, "Bruce, you're a vendor here, and we're one of the biggest companies in the world. You're paid as part of a process; we probably cut a million dollars in checks a day. We can't stop the system for one person."

I did the only thing I could think of: I cashed out the small pension I had, which totalled around $70,000 after penalties—enough with what was in the bank to cover payroll plus a little extra. What I failed to understand at the time was that this was just a band-aid. How would I pay the next month's payroll and the month after that? I wish I had known then what I know now—that this was a cash flow issue. I had to do some critical financial restructuring because of the poor decisions I made and my lack of understanding of how to handle money as a business owner. This was a defining business moment for me.

Even when you think you're taking ownership of everything, blind spots can still catch you off guard. My business was booming, but I had no financial resources in place. I didn't have a relationship with a bank. I didn't have a CPA. More than anything, I was embarrassed. That financial mistake could have cost people their jobs. I had to take responsibility for what happened. So, I set some plans in motion: I hired a CPA and established a banking relationship so I could secure a line of credit and business loans. I learned how to manage the financial side of my business.

Leadership and accountability start at the top. Are you making sure your business is financially stable so your employees aren't worried about losing their jobs? Are you creating an environment where people take pride in coming to work? These are examples of extreme ownership. Own every bit of your responsibility; don't try to put it off on other people. Everybody is responsible for contributing to the overall mission, and it's *your* responsibility as the CEO or business owner to take ownership of your expectations for your company and demonstrate them to your employees.

It's so critical, if you own a business, to have checks and balances in place. You have to regularly check in with your people and ensure everyone is still on the same page. Consider whether your company culture is aligned and if everyone has the same vision. If that's not the case, do everything in your power to remedy that. Problems and misalignment can creep up on you. Say a company gets bigger, and they start to scale, and suddenly they're doing millions of dollars in business, but they're not really talking to each other, and bi-weekly check-ins become superficial. Instead of really finding out how each department is doing, a spreadsheet with some numbers is sent around, and that's it. No communication on goals and setbacks.

The moral of the story here is to always communicate with your people. Ask uncomfortable questions, no matter how big the company gets. Call your customers and ask if they're happy and being treated properly. Solicit feedback and try your hardest to get honest opinions and answers. Because when people are left to their own devices, they will go rogue. You want everyone to be on board with your vision, and if they're not, then they're not a good fit. Sometimes people start out on the same page, only to change. They change their thought process and their philosophy. Perhaps they get greedy or jealous of others' success.

Some people only come into your life for a season, and that's okay. We used to say at Quest Nutrition that, when we were interviewing, we were always looking for the next CEO, but we would settle for an employee. Every time you bring someone into your organization or your company, you hope that they could be your next CEO. You hope that they have a grand vision and that their direction is to see the company rise to greater levels. Nine times out of ten, the people you hire will stay employees, and they may move on from the company long before they get to the executive level. And that's great; everybody needs hard workers. But you should always be looking for the next CEO when you hire—and at the very least for people who align with your vision. When you bring anyone in, you want them to be aligned. But when things change, you have to take ownership of keeping your goals first and foremost and not let anyone alter your mission.

After a long journey at Quest Nutrition, with many ups and downs and people coming and going, the investment firm brought in a new CEO when it invested in Quest. I'll be honest with you. Back then, I didn't understand the complex workings of business. My friends who were entrepreneurs and successful businesspeople/business owners asked me when we were going to sell. I remember telling them that the owners would never sell Quest Nutrition and that it would become a generational company. They all laughed that off. It wasn't until the private equity firm came to the office in person that I understood what it meant to sell a business.

I actually knew the private equity firm because I was friends with the founder. Their goal was ultimately to buy Quest Nutrition and then sell it to a bigger company. One of the founders was removed from the company because his vision was different and was failing miserably. He exited against his will. The other founders, along with the investment firm, decided to bring in a new CEO to clean up the company and get it ready to sell. This was all a foreign language to me. After the new CEO was hired, he evaluated everyone at the company.

I remember getting an email from the new CEO's assistant, whom I knew because she had been someone else's assistant before he joined. The email said that I had an appointment next Tuesday with the CEO and to bring a list of everything I did at the company. I put together this really cool PowerPoint; it was probably nineteen pages too long. One page would've sufficed. I remember the new CEO flipping through all twenty slides in about ten seconds during our meeting. Then he asked me, "What are three things you're going to do moving forward to bring value to this company?"

In that moment, I realized he didn't just want to get to know me or understand what I had accomplished at the company—this was a job interview. That's when it hit me that he was really making changes.

More employees were laid off as the new CEO restructured the company. He started replacing people and bringing in his own team. Shortly after that meeting, I ran into the founder, Ron. He asked how things were going, and I told him that I had a meeting with the new CEO that felt like a job interview. Ron then said, "When the new CEO took over the company, I explained to him that you can get rid of every single person in this company. Every single person. Do whatever you need to do to make this company solid to bring it to market. But you can't get rid of Bruce Cardenas—he's a sacred cow."

I share this quite humbly; I didn't even know what that term meant at the time. Ron said to me, and also to the CEO, that everybody knows me, and a lot of people think I'm the founder. And he highlighted my tremendous pride in Quest Nutrition, calling me the face of the company. He told the CEO it's just not an option to let me go, that I would be the last man standing. I was truly humbled by his endorsement of me. I mention this because I established myself with no self-serving purpose other than to bring value to the company. I traveled forty weekends a year for four years, representing the company at events. Never in a million years did I think I would be part of any kind of exit team or equity pool or in any position of authority. I just had a passion and a desire to help grow the brand.

I am happy to say that I survived the layoffs, and The Simply Good Foods Company acquired Quest Nutrition for one billion dollars in cash. Side note: there have only been 1,100 billion-dollar companies in the entire world. Out of those, just a handful have been cash acquisitions. It was fascinating to be a part of the exit team. I never expected it, but I was qualified and deserving to be included because I had so much pride in the company, and it showed in the ways that *I showed up* every day—to work hard, to go above and beyond, to represent the company with no ego.

People said Quest Nutrition was lightning in a bottle—a once-in-a-lifetime success that reached a billion-dollar valuation because he "got lucky." But luck doesn't strike twice.

I stayed at Quest Nutrition for a year, while simultaneously helping Ron and Michael Veni start Legendary Foods. After that year, I moved to Legendary Foods full-time. We made mistakes at Quest Nutrition, and we had a lot of success, and we learned more than we could've ever imagined. Internally, we call Legendary Foods "Quest Nutrition 2.0," our second billion-dollar company, because we are implementing everything we learned at Quest Nutrition to make Legendary Foods even bigger and better.

Suddenly, the narrative changed. People stopped calling it luck and started calling it leadership, discipline, and vision. They began to understand that Ron has a unique ability to see around corners, to anticipate where consumer needs and nutritional science are heading, and to build teams that execute at the highest level. Ron is proving that billion-dollar outcomes aren't accidents. They're the result of thinking differently, building boldly, and refusing to accept the limits that most people assume are fixed.

Pride and ownership aren't just feel-good concepts. They're fundamental drivers of a strong culture and sustainable business success. When you take extreme ownership of every outcome and create an environment where everyone wants to get behind your mission, you have succeeded as a leader. Collective pride will transform your employees into passionate team members who want to go above and beyond to make the business the best it can be.

As a leader, you have to regularly nurture and monitor the pride and ownership among your employees, keeping everyone positive and determined to succeed. Companies that achieve huge success aren't built by individuals who don't communicate; they're built by teams of people united in their purpose and efforts.

BUSINESS BITES

- **Own everything—and I mean everything.** As a leader, you're responsible for all outcomes, both good and bad. Don't blame others for failures; instead, take accountability for creating the conditions that led to the problems. Make a list of issues you've had (or that you see coming), and make a plan to right the wrongs. Whether it's a financial mess (like when I couldn't make payroll), an unhappy employee, or a product failure, it all comes back to you as the leader.
- **Treat success as a team effort, not a one-person show.** Success requires everyone to buy in and contribute. When you lead by example and support your team, they will want to achieve success as much as you do. If you're a solopreneur, write down a list of your successes to keep you motivated. If you have a team, make it a regular practice to recognize them individually for their contributions to the company's success. Embrace a "we" over "me" mentality, and watch the positive outcomes multiply.
- **Show, don't just tell, when it comes to pride.** When employees see leadership taking ownership through actions rather than just words, it sets the tone for the entire organization. Think of 3-5 tangible ways that you can show pride, such as promoting the right people into leadership positions or regularly having candid conversations with your team. When you step up as a leader and truly live the values

that you say you believe in, that's when real pride starts spreading through your organization.

- **When people take real pride, they become champions of your success.** I've seen it firsthand—when employees truly believe in what you're building, they start thinking of ways to enhance the company's growth on their own. They want to go above and beyond because they're invested in the outcome. Regularly check in with yourself and your team to ensure that everyone is aligned. If people lose their pride and become self-serving—like what happened with some folks at Quest Nutrition—you've got to make tough decisions to protect your values.

Working smarter not harder is a beautiful lie.

You will not know how to work smart until you've worked very hard for an irrationally long time.

– Codie Sanchez

CHAPTER 9
RECLAIMING YOUR HEALTH

From an early age, I carried extra weight. I have vivid memories of playing "shirts and skins" during school basketball games and wishing I could disappear. I would silently beg not to be chosen for "skins," knowing that embarrassment and ridicule would follow. Those insecurities became part of my story and, eventually, the fuel for transformation. Your early struggles can become your lifelong motivation. They are not setbacks, but stepping stones.

As a teenager, I picked up weightlifting, inspired by the physiques I saw in fitness and bodybuilding magazines. Ever since, lifting weights and living a health-conscious lifestyle have been a big part of my life. At one point, I even aspired to follow in the footsteps of Arnold Schwarzenegger. He was a larger-than-life presence who fueled the dreams of countless young athletes like me.

My first real transformation didn't come in a gym, though. It came when I entered the Marine Corps. During the intense training at boot camp, I shed over thirty pounds. More importantly, I discovered discipline, resilience, and the power of the mind to carry the body farther than it ever thought possible.

For well over fifteen years, I maintained a fit, muscular build, weighing 240-250 pounds, with a 36-inch waist. Fast forward to my 40s, and I found myself back at 250 pounds, with a 41-inch waist. I continued to lift weights consistently, but I had neglected my nutrition plan. Looking at photos and videos of myself from various speaking engagements and podcast interviews was a turning point for me. I didn't like what I saw in the photos. I realized I wasn't as healthy as I thought.

Not long after this realization, I reconnected with my good friend, Carl Ferro, who founded Sunfare, a Los Angeles-based company that offers healthy meal prep services and nationwide delivery. Carl got me set up with a meal plan. At the time this book was printed, I had just completed a 90-day program and a 60-pound body transformation. Think about that: I was carrying the equivalent of a 60-pound dumbbell everywhere I went—up and down stairs, into meetings, day in and day out. That extra weight was putting a lot of wear and tear on my musculoskeletal system and, most importantly, my cardiovascular system. I am now back at my high school wrestling weight.

I finally figured out that my optimum weight is directly tied to diet and nutrition, not just working hard in the gym. That meal prep service is still part of my lifestyle today; I'm living for the long game. Carl's service changed my life in ways I couldn't have imagined. It has changed so many aspects of my life—not only how I look, but how I feel. This wasn't just about losing weight; it was about reclaiming my health, my confidence, and my future.

I eliminated sleep apnea, acid reflux, and high blood pressure. I now wake every morning before 5 a.m., full of energy, clarity, and focus. My lifestyle has changed completely: no artificial sweeteners, sauces, creams, or processed foods—only whole, clean nutrition.

It was time to truly live the lifestyle I owed not only to myself, but also to my family and loved ones. My father passed away from colon cancer at an age that was far too young by any measure. I have since outlived that age, and his passing serves as a daily reminder that life is fragile and health is priceless.

Spending time with the team in the early days of Quest, we realized that we would all, at some point, be affected by cancer or heart disease, either directly or indirectly. So, in 2015, Ron Penna brought in a cardiologist and his team to do some preliminary testing on any employee who volunteered for a free heart screening. I took advantage of the gracious offer. The initial screening led to more in-depth screening for me. After extensive testing, the doctors discovered that I had an 80 percent blockage in one of the main arteries in my heart, known as the "widowmaker" because a near-complete blockage of this artery can be fatal. They put in a stent to open up the obstruction. This ultimately saved my life, as I never would have thought I needed to undergo a screening like that.

Fast forward to 2025 and even more innovative thinking: I had more advanced testing done with the Cleerly test, only to discover that I had 75% blockage in another of my main arteries. Confronted with my own mortality, I'm addressing this with specialists that focus on heart attack and stroke prevention with an aggressive protocol and treatments.

I share this with you because on the outside, I look healthy. I work out 7 days a week. I shared what I discovered with some of my friends, in hopes of encouraging them to check their own hearts. They told me that they get their regular annual physicals and that they always get a clean bill of health. An annual physical would never have discovered the blockages that I have. Basic testing paid for by insurance, unfortunately, is not enough.

While the news was sobering, it reminded me that although we can't control every aspect of our health, we can control how we respond. We can choose to be proactive, informed, and intentional about how we care for ourselves.

Proactive health goes beyond individual choices, which is why the medical research side of Legendary Foods is so important. For about a decade, Ron has personally funded millions of dollars for cancer and heart disease research. It is an important part of our mission to give back through funding privatized scientific research.

We recently decided to start our own foundation, **BioShift Research Foundation**, a nonprofit organization 100 percent focused on finding answers and cures for both cancer and heart disease. We now have almost 15,000 square feet of laboratories, with scientists, technicians, and physicians all working tirelessly to find answers for the prevention of cancer, heart disease, and other metabolic diseases. We are committed to progressing the fields of cancer diagnostics and early detection, with an emphasis on triple negative breast cancer, as well as cardiovascular disease reversal and prevention, among other goals. Our team has many years of combined experience across scientific, medical, and biomedical fields.

I'm proud to be a part of this organization and can truly say that I'm fortunate to have found another "why" and purpose in my life.

If you would like to learn more, visit bioshiftresearchfoundation.org. I hope you will follow me and our amazing team on our journey.

Alongside prioritizing this research mission for the future, I also know that each of us has to own our individual health journey right now. We can't just wait for future breakthroughs; we have to take care of ourselves today.

My mission now is not to chase quick fixes or dramatic transformations, but to commit to the long game: a life built on consistent choices, healthy habits, and a fitness-driven mindset that will carry me through every day I'm blessed to live. I share all of this because I hope it inspires reflection.

No matter what stage of life you're in, it's never too late to get on track with your fitness and health journey; in fact, it's your most important investment. Life is incredibly short, and as we move through our 40s, 50s, and 60s, friends and loved ones begin to pass away from obesity, heart disease, and other metabolic-related conditions.

If you're unsure where to begin your health and fitness journey, remember this: just start. Start with one step, one movement, and one meal at a time. Track it all with one of the many free apps available right on your phone. If you're an all-or-nothing kind of person like me, then commit fully to that first step. I committed to Carl at

Sunfare Meals, and I followed the process without wavering. There was no secret formula to my success. No biohacking. No miracle drugs.

My daily routine is simple. I wake up at the same time every morning, drink sixteen ounces of water on the way to the gym, and complete a straightforward, full-body workout—mostly cables and dumbbells. I'm usually finished in under forty minutes.

To break it down to its simplest explanation, it all comes down to:

Diet. Exercise. Mindset.

Do I still get cravings for sweets or a big, greasy cheeseburger? Of course I do. And when those cravings hit, I often turn to Legendary Foods because I believe in the products I work hard to put out into the world. I enjoy the healthier alternatives offered in both sweet and savory categories. Do I still eat out occasionally, enjoying a pizza or burger? Yes. But here's the key: The very next day, I'm back on track. I don't let one "cheat meal" turn into a second, then a third, until the pounds start creeping back on. That's the trap I refuse to fall into again.

Your journey is yours to own. Every choice you make compounds over time. What you eat, how you move, how you care for your body, how you manage stress. It all counts. Stay focused, my friends. Don't wait for a wake-up call. Commit, trust the process, and take that first step toward the life you deserve. Live with discipline, but also with joy. When you live a healthy lifestyle, you're not just adding years to your life—you're adding life to your years.

This is about more than your personal health; these habits influence how you operate as a leader. Leaders who maintain physical fitness have statistically higher employee retention and loyalty. I saw this first-hand from the founders at Quest. Shannon competed in bodybuild-ing, and Ron has always maintained the highest level of physical fitness. At Quest, we offered free gym memberships, in-house biohacking services, tanning beds, sleeping rooms, massages, and therapy and bodywork treatments—all complimentary for employees.

We brought these same offerings to Legendary Foods. Many employees have been inspired to reflect and work on their own wellness journey because they see the good we are doing with our products and health research. Nothing is mandated or even verbally encouraged, but when people see others taking care of themselves and the results that follow, it creates a ripple effect. Many members of our team wear Oura Rings, utilize mouth taping at night, chew resistance gum, and regularly use tanning beds for exposure.

As leaders, we can't pour from an empty cup. Taking care of your health isn't selfish—it's foundational. When you lead from a healthy fitness mindset, you set a standard for others to follow and expand your impact. There are countless ways to prioritize health as a leader: mentoring others, creating a wellness-focused culture, or supporting health initiatives in your community. We only have one life. Show up fully for yourself and those who depend on you. That's what being a successful leader means.

BUSINESS BITES

- **Your personal health directly impacts your effectiveness as a leader.** Not being the healthiest version of myself for so long began to wear on me, and it affected how I performed as a leader. I went from struggling through the day with high blood pressure and sleep apnea to waking up before sunrise full of energy, clarity, and focus. When I transformed my health, I also transformed my leadership capabilities. You can't lead others effectively if you're not taking care of your physical and mental well-being.
- **Invest in your people's health.** Wellness programs aren't just feel-good initiatives. Those free heart screenings for Quest Nutrition employees were more than just a nice gesture—that was an investment in the health of the team. Prioritizing employee health keeps your best people well-rested, focused, and showing up every day ready to give it their all.

- **Find a purpose beyond your paycheck.** I know I've stated this before, but it's an important one. What can you do or create that can be part of your legacy and purpose? When you build or contribute to something that genuinely helps people, it gives your work deeper meaning beyond just making money. That purpose fuels everything you do.

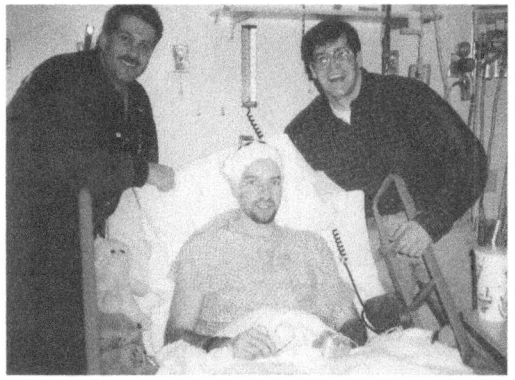

With my brother Brian in the hospital, who later passed away from brain cancer, and my younger brother Jimmy. Brian is one of the reasons I'm so committed to the Bio Shift Research Foundation.

From my time working as a personal trainer at Gold's Gym before joining the LAPD

Working out with Nicole Bass in NYC

Before the transformation—250 lbs, XXL

Health and fitness: a journey that never ends

Strength training becomes increasingly important as we age

New beginnings after losing 55+ pounds

CONCLUSION

If you've made it this far, you've invested time in yourself—and that investment matters. The principles in this book aren't just concepts to understand; they're tools to implement at any stage of your personal or professional journey. Let's recap them:

1. **Anchor yourself in purpose:** Having an overall vision is the compass that guides the direction of your life.
2. **Discover the "why" that drives you:** Your why is the motivator that keeps you focused on fulfilling your purpose.
3. **Lead by serving others:** True leadership isn't about power— it's about service. A servant leader listens, uplifts, and leads by example.
4. **Master the art of connection:** Communication is the backbone of any successful venture. A good leader listens with the intent to understand.
5. **Develop relationship capital:** Relationships are your greatest form of currency. When you invest in others, expecting nothing in return, you create bonds that last.
6. **Transform interactions into opportunities:** Every conversation is a chance to learn, connect, or create value. Be

open and willing to take a risk; you never know where your
daily encounters might lead.

7. **Build discipline and work ethic:** Vision without execution
   is just a dream. Focus on the task at hand and see it through
   to completion.

8. **Own your work to own your success:** Pride in what you do
   translates to every aspect of your work. Your contribution
   matters; give it your best effort.

9. **Reclaim your health:** Health is about discipline and
   consistency when it comes to nutrition and exercise. It's
   worth it in the long run to take care of your health.

———

Living these principles daily has opened doors I never imagined
possible. While almost every one of these unique opportunities has
been work-related—whether providing personal protection for clients
or serving as a police officer—each experience has been extraordinary,
and some truly once-in-a-lifetime.

Here's a glimpse of what I've been fortunate to experience:

Attended 22 Super Bowls
Attended 12 World Series championships
Attended 3 NBA championships
Visited the White House five times
Attended 3 World Cup soccer championships
Visited the Vatican with a client to meet the Pope
Visited the Western Wall in Jerusalem on three separate occasions with clients
Worked and attended multiple times with clients: the
Academy Awards, the Golden Globes, the Emmys, the
Country Music Awards, and countless concerts and live
performances

I've been in rooms that made me reflect on just how unique this journey has been. I share this not to boast, but to express humble gratitude for the life I've lived so far and the position I am in.

———

I wrote this book to help you see the potential in yourself and others to grow and shine and to encourage you to take action on a dream or a goal. I'm a prime example that anything and everything is possible. My only hope is that this book brings you value and helps you take even a small step forward on your journey to becoming an entrepreneur or being a better CEO, employee, or person.

Thank you for being on this journey with me and for taking the time out of your busy life to read this book. My writing journey is far from over; this is, hopefully, my first book of many. There are still a lot of lessons to be learned in this life, and I want to be able to share them through my writing and speaking engagements. I'm looking forward to the next chapter in my journey, and I look forward to having you with me.

Love & Respect,
Bruce

BRUCE'S BOARDROOM PLAYBOOK

Making it into boardrooms isn't about having the most impressive resume or a polished pitch to perfection. It's about showing up ready to put yourself out there to solve problems and add value before you ask for anything in return. This is my top twenty list of advice for understanding what it takes to be in a boardroom.

1. The room you're in determines your next level.
2. You can't build a business through DMs alone.
3. Your Rolodex is more valuable than your pitch deck.
4. If you don't know what you need, we can't help you.
5. Contribution first—that's how this room works.
6. Your failures are where your real value lives.
7. We don't have members. We have Advisors.
8. It's not a table; it's the Board.
9. Clarity builds trust. Conviction makes deals happen.
10. This isn't networking; it's acceleration.
11. The fastest path to ROI is giving first.
12. If you sit on the Board, you'd better be ready to contribute.
13. This isn't a waiting room. This is a working room.
14. You already have the wins. Now give them away.
15. You don't need more time. You need more clarity.
16. This is the room that rewrites your story.
17. When you're all in, people can feel it.
18. Compression creates connection. That's the power of the Board.
19. One introduction can change everything.
20. This isn't inspiration. It's activation.

BRUCEISMS

Anyone who has spent any time around me has heard these sayings of mine. I repeat them until people are probably sick of hearing them because they work. These aren't motivation quotes to stick on a wall and forget about; these are principles that I live by—ones that I have learned the hard way in some cases, have saved me a lot of wasted time, and that have brought me success in my business.

1. Be on time! That means 15 minutes early!
2. Never show up empty-handed.
3. Bring value with NO ask in return.
4. Take pride in ownership.
5. You are going to run out of time. Do it today.
6. Be prepared for any unexpected storm.
7. Don't just meet people's expectations, but exceed them.
8. Trust everybody, but verify.
9. Believe nothing on social media.
10. When wealthy people tell you to follow your passion, they forget to tell you they made their wealth doing things that had nothing to do with their passion.
11. Do not borrow money or bring in private equity unless it's an absolute must.
12. Do you want to buy an exotic car? Use TURO and rent someone else's vehicle and get it out of your system.
13. Don't make spontaneous life-changing decisions. Always take 24 hours to think through the process.
14. Find a charity and support it.
15. Do not take advice from people who don't have the lives you want.

LIFE COMPASS LESSONS

These principles have guided my decisions, shaped my personal and professional relationships, and helped define my purpose. They remind me that success isn't just about achievements; it's about the people that I help and the legacy that I leave behind. This is my compass for leading a life of intention, generosity, and impact.

1. Live a life of making more deposits than withdrawals.
2. ROE: return on energy.
3. I help brands build culture and become a magnetic (PULL) product and not a (PUSH) product.
4. Life doesn't happen to you, but for you.
5. HOPE: Help One Person Each day.
6. Going broke after investing is not the same as going broke after impressing.
7. Money will find you if you make helping people your mission.
8. Excuses will always be there for you, opportunity won't.
9. Don't worry about your brand; worry about your products and the buying experience for your customers.
10. Sell the benefits, not the features.
11. The magic you were looking for is in the work you are avoiding.
12. A candle loses nothing by lighting other candles.
13. The power of proximity. Be around mentors.
14. Your net worth is your network.
15. Spend more time with people who inspire you to think bigger.
16. Be generous with your time.
17. Be respectful to all.
18. Be hard to kill.

19. Be easy to love.
20. Be ready with a plan.
21. Be kind with your words.
22. Be protective of your reputation.
23. Be open to growth

COMPANIES I SUPPORT

The following are companies where I serve as either an investor or a partner, or companies whose brand I truly enjoy and want to share with you.

Legendary Foods

    https://www.eatlegendary.com/

Bio Shift Research Foundation

    https://www.bioshiftresearchfoundation.org/

Good Nutrition Only

    https://goodnutritiononly.com

Perfy Drinks

    https://drinkperfy.com/

SunFare Meals

    https://sunfare.com/

California Ice Protein

    https://www.californiaiceprotein.com/

ACKNOWLEDGEMENTS

To Sarah, Nick (Bruce), and Leslie, I'm very proud of each of you for your accomplishments in this life. Much love, Dad.

Albert and Arnold Gasparri, the founders of A&A Market in High Bridge, N.J. You gave me my first real job when I was a young teenager. Thanks for holding me accountable and teaching me about work ethic.

To the men of the High Bridge Police Department. Thank you for the opportunity to ride along after school. That made me feel like I was part of the police department as an auxiliary police officer. Thank you, Chief Lacey, for giving me the advice to go into the Marine Corps.

To Sergeants Thompson, Hummel, and Finn of the United States Marine Corps, Parris Island. I will never forget each of you for transforming me from a boy into a man in a short time.

To Mike Graber, it was an honor to be your number one car sales agent for an entire year while I went through the process to become a police officer.

To my first training officer, Bob, who taught me life's lessons you can't learn in school.

To Officer Williams, who later retired as a captain with the LAPD. You were tough on me, and I learned a lot about resilience.

To Mr. Perelman, my first and longest client for my executive protection business. One tough entrepreneur and one of the original billionaires.

To Charlie Horky, the founder of CLS Transportation. You were instrumental in opening doors and making connections to grow my executive protection business.

To Ron and Shannan Penna, the founders of Quest Nutrition. We're well into our second decade working together, and I can honestly say I've learned more from Ron than I can express—not only about the nutrition industry but also about science and business philosophies, too. You are a self-taught man. You read and study ferociously for knowledge, and we have spent thousands of hours talking, learning, and growing together. I am beyond grateful that you keep giving me opportunities to discover new meaning and purpose in my life. I have a feeling that by the time you pick up this book, we'll be thinking about our third unicorn—and starting that next side hustle. A serendipitous encounter at the gym changed the trajectory of my life; thank you both.

THANK YOU FOR READING MY BOOK!

LET'S CONNECT!
Scan the QR Code:

I appreciate your interest in my book and value your feedback, as it helps me improve future versions of this book.
I would appreciate it if you could leave your invaluable review on Amazon.com with your feedback.
Thank you!